Winning Big
The Life, Loves, Times and TIPS of Contest Queen Carol Shaffer

Colin J. Mitchell

Manor House Publishing
www.manor-house.biz
905-648-2193

Library and Archives Canada Cataloguing in Publication

Mitchell, Colin, 1987-
  Winning big : the life, loves, times and tips of contest queen Carol
Shaffer / Colin Mitchell.

ISBN 978-1-897453-02-5

  1. Shaffer, Carol. 2. Contests. 3. Contests--United States--Biography.
I. Title.

GV1201.6.M58 2008   790.1'34092
C2008-905962-X

First Edition.
192 pages.
All rights reserved.

Cover design: Michael B. Davie and Donovan Davie
Cover photos, front and back, courtesy of Karen Allen, Allen Fine Art Photography, 709 Brackett St. Swansea, IL 62226 USA
314-442-5528 For more information: mystlouisphotographer.com

Published September 30, 2008
Manor House Publishing Inc.
www.manor-house.biz
(905) 648-2193

We gratefully acknowledge the financial support of the Government of Canada through the Book Publishing Industry Development Program (BPIDP), Dept. of Canadian Heritage, for our publishing activities.

Manor House Publishing Inc.
www.manor-house.biz
905-648-2193

1

Walter Wright dabbed his brow, then gently wiped stinging sweat from the eyes of his panting, very pregnant wife Wilma.

Glenn Miller's *Moon Love* played low on the radio but this was a very Earthbound and stifling hot corridor at St. Mary's Hospital in East St. Louis, Illinois, August 7, 1939.

As Wilma was wheeled into the delivery room, a nun rushed ahead to make sure the drapes were fully drawn; a futile effort to block out the blistering summer sun. But there was no air conditioner, no fan, no escape from the blanketing, sweltering heat that smothered the room.

Wilma had joked if there'd been a contest over the gender of her coming first child, she'd win. Now, drenched in sweat, deep in labour, Wilma knew she'd won: She was giving birth to a girl. Her daughter would bear the unusual name of Caroleen Ruth Wright, a special name for a special girl, destined for an unusual life... a contest-winner was born...

As the Wrights drove back to their home in the nearby leafy little town of Maplewood Park, they grinned at the newborn Caroleen asleep on her mother's lap and reflected on their own lives.

Wilma, the only child of Otis and Ora Gray, was born in Chester, Illinois, but at age 3 moved with her parents to enjoy a quiet life at Maplewood Park.

In contrast, Walter hailed from Columbia, Tennessee, was the fourth of seven children, and his life was far from uneventful: When he was 10, his mother died from tuberculosis shortly after giving birth to twin girls. One of the babies died. The other, Francis, survived but had severe cerebral palsy. His father moved the family to Springhill, TN, and the children were separated and placed with various relatives. Still grieving the loss of his mother, Walter soon came to feel alone and unwanted as he was shuffled from one relative to another, eventually winding up in Nashville. The emotional scars never healed and a dark side festered in Walter that would eventually be revealed with tragic consequences.

Walter dropped out of Grade 8 and worked several unskilled jobs before arriving in Maplewood Park in 1938, at age 20, to board with a relative, Cliff Latta, and work for his heating coal delivery business.

During a coal delivery to 733 Mildred Avenue, Walter came upon the pretty 17-year-old Wilma, who found him the "most handsome man," she'd ever seen. It was a fair assessment: Nearly six feet tall, Walter had a well tAnnd muscular build, tousled hair streaked blond from the sun and "gorgeous blue eyes that twinkled when he laughed." Sparks flew.

Wilma's parents however were far from impressed. Ora claimed he came a-courting barefoot, though Wilma disputed this. No one denies he drove up for a date in an old Model-T Ford in dire need of a paint job. But Wilma and her girlfriends soon made it shine with bright yellow paint.

Wilma was a gifted musician, and on graduating from Dupo High School, won a music scholarship and was promised a music instructor job after she completed her studies. But she never took advantage of this opportunity.

Deeply in love with Walter, she decided to forego school in the fall of 1938 and instead eloped with Walter to St. Charles, Missouri, where they were married by a Justice of the Peace. Her size-3 peach-colored prom dress served as her wedding gown.

The newlyweds honeymooned in a boarding house before moving into Walter's room next to a barn at Cliff Latta's coal delivery business.

Soon after, the coal business was sold to man with sons and Walter was no longer needed. He got a watchman's job on the levee along the Mississippi River paying $20 per week and free housing, but he had to kick back $5 to keep the job. To supplement his income he also dug ditches and graves.

One day he heard about a job paying $40 a week at the Aluminum Ore plant in E. St. Louis. He found out where the job supervisor lived and went to the man's house several times until he found him at home. The supervisor was so impressed with Walter's persistence that he hired him.

After Caroleen's arrival, Walter became a bricklayer and repaired the Aluminum Ore plant smoke stacks. Occasionally he'd find a pigeon's nest at the top of one of the smoke stacks, with baby pigeons in the nest. Other workers would throw the nests and the chicks to the ground, but Walter would put the tiny birds in his pockets and bring them home where he and Wilma hand fed them until they were big enough to be on their own.

In 1942, when Caroleen was 3, her only sibling, Jo Ann, was born and the young family rented a small frame 3-room house on Mildred Avenue with a red picket fence – and an outhouse out back. There was no running water. Wilma had to pump water and heat the water for dishes and bathing. The home's saving grace was that it was on the same street as Wilma's parents. With World War II raging, Walter expected to be drafted at any time and wanted his family close by the children's grandparents.

Despite wartime, Caroleen enjoyed an idyllic early childhood. Walter earned enough money to enroll her in tap dancing lessons at the Mary Louise Dance School followed by ice cream sodas at a Woolworth's Dime Store. "I loved tap dancing," Caroleen recalls. "I was only 3 when I started… I liked the noise the tap shoes made…." She would fondly recollect the experience many years later as a contestant in the Ms Illinois American Senior Classic Pageant – and would win the talent portion of the pageant with her tap routine.

2

At age 5, Caroleen was already beginning to be referred to as "Carol" although it would be many years later before she changed her name to Carol.

That same year, her dad received the dreaded U.S. Army draft notice: to fight, and possibly die, in the Pacific. "He didn't want to go," Carol recalls, "but he only had one week to get things in order and then catch a troop train at Union Station in St. Louis, Missouri. Grand-Pa Gray drove him there, and Mom, Jo Ann, Grand-Ma Gray, and I went along to see him off. Before he got on the train he kissed us good bye... even kissed Grand-Ma Gray. There were tears in his eyes and that is the only time I ever saw my Dad cry. Later he would say that it was because he kissed his mother-in-law that day that his luck went sour."

After basic training at Little Rock, Arkansas, Walter shipped out for Japan. The whole crew was badly seasick but jubilant when they learned the Japanese had surrendered on Sept. 2, 1945, after the U.S. dropped an atomic bomb on Hiroshima. The soldiers' role was now one of reconstruction. Walter drove a bulldozer, rebuilt roads... and wrote letters to loved ones back home...

"Dad wrote many letters describing his life in Japan," Carol recalls. "I liked hearing about a pet monkey he had, and in one of his letters he included a picture of him holding the monkey. He said he was going to bring the monkey home with him... but he wasn't allowed to take him."

Carol cherished her father's letters over his 30-month term of service in Japan. Although he could not attend her sixth and seventh birthdays, his kind and loving image frequently filled her thoughts. She knew him at that time as a wonderful, devoted father. "Before he went into the army he was a cheerful, happy-go-lucky fellow. He whistled a lot; he hardly ever drank; I never heard him say a cross word to Mom; and, if I had a terrible ear ache he would blow cigar smoke into my ear to make it feel better."

What Carol could not have known was that the years her father spent in a hostile country had changed him into a mean, hardened drinker.

Despite Japan's unconditional surrender, it was still dangerous for American military stationed there as Walter discovered when his best friend was shot and killed by a Japanese sniper as the two pals were walking down a street. The horrific, traumatic experience of his friend collapsing dead at his feet caused lasting psychological damage to the young man who'd lost his mother and spent much of his youth unwanted, and living in strange towns without friends or siblings. Now his best friend lay dead and he was alone in a land of hostile strangers. He became nervous and jittery, prone to punching anyone who came up behind him unexpectedly. He coped with his pain by getting lost in an alcoholic haze.

On an otherwise ordinary day at Maplewood Grade School, Carol looked up from her Grade 2 studies to see principal Cliff Latta Jr. – son of the former coal business owner and her relative – stride into the classroom and whisper in the teacher's ear. Miss Miller smiled and announced: "Carol, you are excused from class today. Your father is home."

Carol remembers well the feeling of pure joy that filled her that day:

"I couldn't believe it... my Dad was home! I lived close to the school and ran all the way home saying to myself, 'Daddy's home...Daddy's home!' When I got to my house I saw that the front yard was full of people... relatives and friends. Even though Dad was from Tennessee, and Mom was from Illinois, he had more relatives living in Maplewood Park than Mom. I saw Charley Bess, proprietor of Bess's Grocery Store, greeting Dad, handsome in his army uniform. Everyone was laughing and patting Dad on his back while Mom was clutching one of his arms. He was holding Jo Ann with his other arm – she was squirming to get down. Although she had his features, they never bonded – Dad was a stranger to her as she was a toddler when he left. And he'd wanted a boy when she was born."

Carol found the chaotic scene overwhelming.

"With all the commotion at my house I suddenly felt shy and I hesitated at the gate. Suddenly Dad saw me and handed my sister to Mom. He ran to where I was standing, scooped me up, gave me a big hug and asked, 'Are you still my gal?' Then, I didn't feel shy any more, just extremely happy. It was a glorious day because my Daddy was home. That evening supper was a feast of the many dishes that people had brought to our house to welcome a hero home. When Dad returned to his job at Aluminum Ore everyone there was happy to see him too…"

The fanfare faded in the days and weeks that followed, but life never returned to normal for the Wright family. Walter was becoming more and more restless and discontent with his life… and drinking heavily.

"On weekends he would invite several of his relatives for dinner, insisting that Mom do it up good," Carol recalls. "Later, I'd hear my folks arguing because Mom had spent too much money on groceries. Mom would fire back with, 'What do you expect? We're feeding the Lattas!' It frightened me when I'd hear them fighting. Sometimes when they'd have one of their arguments Dad would slam out of the house, shouting that he was going to the Maplewood Tavern to 'cool-off'."

After Walter repeatedly complained about paying rent to "Old Man Moreno," he and Wilma managed to save enough to buy a two-acre lot – priced at just $1,000 as it was close to the railroad tracks that ran through town. With their lot paid for, they got a construction loan to build a house. Walter now had a project to occupy his free time. Every night after dinner he'd walk to the lot and work until dark digging out the basement, wearing out several shovels in the process. Then, Wilma helped him mix and pour the concrete floor and lay the concrete block walls.

Carol and her sister Jo Ann always went with their parents to the building site. There they met future next door neighbors, and made friends with Waldo and Dorothy Walker's children: Jimmy, who was Carol's age; and Ruth Ann, who was Jo Ann's age. Due to politics, Waldo, a Republican, and Walter, a die-hard Democrat, never became friends.

With help from some of Walter's relatives and from Grand-Pa Gray, the frame and roof were erected in a couple of days, Carol recalls.

"While the men worked, the women prepared food... everyone was laughing and enjoying the camaraderie..."

Although small – just two bedrooms, a living room, kitchen and bathroom – the newly built house was a mansion compared to the little rented house they'd left behind. And the new home had indoor plumbing!

Wilma loved her new house and kept it spotless – she didn't allow neighborhood kids inside for fear they'd mark up her wood floors. She would sing as she cleaned or cooked – and she was admired for the Southern-style cooking skills she'd learned from Walter's Aunt Winnie.

Carol made friends throughout the new neighbourhood, and became good friends with classmate Barbara Borders. "She lived about two blocks from my house in the nicest house in the neighbourhood..." But the friendship was short-lived: Just as politics had prevented friendship between her father and a neighbor, adult "values" would soon unfairly end the natural, unconditional friendship between the two children.

"I loved to go to Barbara's house to play," Carol recalls, "until the day her mother told me: 'I don't want you playing with Barbara anymore. Go home...you don't talk right.' I had inherited my father's Southern drawl, and apparently she didn't like my accent... I never went to Barbara's house again..."

Oddly enough, Carol's father would pay the Borders a visit – of sorts. Walter had been drinking heavily one day when he challenged the neighborhood kids to a foot race around the neighborhood. He took a shortcut through Borders' yard, tripped on a crochet hoop and fell flat on his face in front of the Borders. They were not amused.

Walter provided another humorous moment when he decided to make homemade headcheese by first butchering a pig the way his relatives in Tennessee did. He brought a pig home and put it in the basement where he plAnnd to butcher it, then got a knife and went down to the basement. The neighbors were alarmed by high-pitched squeals from the basement and feared something bad was happening to the Wright children. On peering through the basement window, Waldo Walker saw "my Dad chasing a pig with a knife and the pig squealing to high heaven," Carol recalls with a laugh.

But such moments of comic relief were few from a father whose drinking was spiraling out of control.

"We hadn't been in our new house a year," Carol recalls, "when Dad became discontented with this house and complained that he didn't know why he built a frame house instead of a brick house. 'After all,' he said, 'I'm a bricklayer. I should have a brick house.' Mom reminded him that they built the frame house because lumber was cheaper than bricks... Mom told him she loved the house and accused Dad of trying to keep up with his more affluent relatives... they were always fighting..."

Carol recollects one particularly disturbing time that marked the beginning a very troubled period in her life: "When Mom said she'd never sign the papers to sell the house, Dad left in a huff, slamming the door and shouting that he was going to Maplewood Tavern to 'cool off.' He had been cooling off quite often, not only at The Maplewood Tavern, but also at Wilson's Tavern, Sudberry's Tavern, and The Shack. That night he came home falling-down drunk. He slapped Mom and pulled her hair... and this was the beginning of the dark era of my life."

Witnessing her father beat her mother was a horrifying experience that forever shattered her childhood image of a tender and loving dad.

"It was as if I had two Dads... the sober one who was kind and loved animals, and the drunk who was mean and scary. There were many scary incidents that could be terrifying..."

As a child living an abusive home life, she found refuge elsewhere. One such means of escape lay in business enterprises she concocted. "My sister and I were always trying to figure out ways to make money," Carol reminisces, "as often this was the only way I could get something I wanted or needed. When there's an alcoholic in the family, money is in short supply because that person spends his money on alcohol for himself or for rounds of drinks at the taverns. My mother could barely pay the bills, so there wasn't any extra money, so I turned to contesting and enterprises."

She recalls one enterprising moment in particular: "We lived close to a railroad track... trains would be stopped for as long as 30 to 45 minutes and the people waiting in the automobiles for the train to pass would be hot and thirsty – this was before automobiles had air conditioning. My sister, our friend Ruth Ann Walker, and I, would mix up two or three pitchers of cold Kool-Aid, put the Kool-Aid and some drinking glasses in a wagon and go to where the cars were stopped. We had a captive row of customers buying Kool-Aid for 25 cents a glass..."

But the main place of refuge was school. "Because of the horrors at home I looked forward to school more and more," Carol recollects. "At school I received the attention and praise that I craved, but wasn't getting at home...

My favorite classes at school were geography and art. I loved to read about exotic places like China, Australia, Russia, Europe, Greece, Canada, Hawaii, Croatia..." Little did Carol know that she would one day visit all of those places and more, thanks to her skill at winning contests.

It was at school, in Grade 3, that Carol entered and won her first-ever contest – by paying close attention to detail and giving the contest-holder exactly what was wanted, an approach she would use with great success throughout her life.

Carol's art teacher had announced a drawing/coloring contest.

"She said we could draw and color whatever we wished," Carol recalls, "but she urged us to try to remember what she had taught us through the year. She said a prize, a box of crayons, would go to the best artist. Also the winning picture would be displayed in the main hall near the Principal's office. She told us how wonderful it would be that everyone who visited the school would see it."

Starved for attention and eager to please her teacher, Carol focused on winning the contest. It was a wonderful escape, a fantasy of victory...

"That night I could hardly go to sleep for thinking about the contest. I kept searching my mind with everything our teacher had taught us about the color wheel and about how certain colors complement each other. She taught us how to use bold colors in contrast with pastels. She said not to make a picture too busy and how to enhance art work and make it more interesting by using various art mediums. As I tried to come up with an idea for my entry I remembered her saying: 'A sky is never all blue, nor is water all blue.' I knew what I would draw... a waterfall that would have both sky and water and I would be sure not to color them all blue."

Carol was jubilant when the contest outcome was announced:

"I won! What a great feeling it was to be a winner. The teacher smiled at me, and the other students looked at me with envy. Winning the art contest made a profound impact on me because it made me feel special and important, gave me a feeling of confidence and self worth. I still have that 'goose-bumps' feeling today whenever I or one of my children or grandchildren win a contest or sweepstakes. I believe it is important for contesting enthusiasts to be creative and also competitive... but not be discouraged if they don't succeed. There is always another day... another contest or sweepstakes to enter! To this day I will try my darnedest to win and it doesn't matter what the prize is. It's the thrill of winning something that has a hold on me."

Carol's next experience as a contest winner would follow soon after as a Grade 4 student at Maplewood Grade School. Her teacher announced a talent show was taking place at Maplewood and at each of the other four schools in the district. There would be one boy and one girl winner from each school. The winners from the five schools would then perform on stage at the Maplewood Movie Theater where a grand prize winner would be chosen. The prize: $25 and a pair of movie tickets.

She decided to enter the talent competition with a tap dance routine.

"I no longer took dance lessons because my mother couldn't afford to send me, but I still knew some of my routines. I only hoped my costume and shoes would fit..."

Rummaging through a cedar chest, Carol found a dress and white tap shoes and tried them on. "The dress, a short, white satin dress trimmed in silver sequins, was snug but it still fit – it was good I was a skinny kid. The shoes were stretched and worn, but they fit. The dress was somewhat wrinkled, but it would have to do. I couldn't ask Mom to iron the dress because I didn't want her or Dad to know I was entering the talent show in case I didn't do well."

Carol recounts what happened next: "Contestants had to perform alphabetically, so with the last name of Wright this meant I would be last. I have found that sometimes this is good because the last performer is most likely to be remembered by the judges. I won! As the girl winner from my school I'd be competing for the Grand Prize that coming Friday at the Maplewood Movie Theater. My parents were flabbergasted when they heard I had won a talent show. They didn't know I could still dance. That Friday we walked to the theater, and during the intermission all finalists where called back stage. Mr. Latta served as the MC for the contest, and after all the contestants had performed he had us come back on stage where he held his hand over each performer's head. The audience would vote by applauding for the performer they liked best."

The applause for Carol was deafening. She tied with little Timmy Stewart, also a tap dancer, for the Grand Prize. Many years later Carol would recall this experience after winning a part as an extra in a Hollywood movie – before going on to appear in several more movies.

"I believe I won the talent contest because I was the only performer in costume... I stood out and was noticed. It's a strategy I've used many times: I won a Mexican cooking contest after dressing in a Mexican outfit; I won a cookie baking contest with my 'cowgirl' cookies after dressing in Western attire so I'd be noticed. This strategy can apply with entry blanks as well. Many times I will decorate an entry that I drop in a box or an envelope or a post card so they will stand out and hopefully be chosen."

3

While Carol basked in the limelight of her newfound talent, she'd inevitably return to a bleak and abusive life at home. "Alcoholism was slowly stealing our Dad away from my sister and me," Carol notes. "He was drinking more and more, especially on weekends... I never knew what Dad might do. If he had a confrontation, or argument with someone at a bar this could set him off and he would come home and take it out on Mom and sometimes Jo Ann and me too."

There was another problem that was more subtle. "It seemed that the more Dad drank, the more Mom ate. She turned to food for comfort and had put on an enormous amount of weight, wore a size 18 1/2 dress. Dad had something else he could gripe at her about... her weight. He was abusive not only physically, but verbally as well. He'd make fun of Mom, tell her she was fat and ugly. I would think to myself, *I sure hope I never get fat.* It seemed like getting fat was some kind of a terrible sin."

Her father's drunken, abstract anger was thrown in all directions, including Wilma's accomplishment of completing a successful education.

"Dad was jealous that Mom had graduated from high school and he hadn't finished the eighth grade," Carol remembers, "He was very good at math, especially figuring how many bricks would be needed per square foot for a particular structure ... He would get Mom out of bed when he came home late and make her figure out the number of bricks needed for a house. When he did this she would be so nervous she could hardly think and would invariably come up with the wrong answer. Then he would really make fun of her education."

Carol's mother inevitably began to lose her self-confidence and sense of security in their fragile family life. Things only became worse when another couple who enjoyed a drink befriended Walter, much to the dismay of his wife.

Paul and Dotty Baggett became regular guests at the family home, recalls Carol...

"Mom didn't drink, but to please Dad she, Jo Ann and I would go to the bars with them. The Baggetts had two daughters, Jane and Ann, the same ages as Jo Ann and I."

Paul Baggett was a happy drunk who loved to sing endless rounds of Irish drinking tunes with Walter over an evening at the pub, but his wife Dotty was just the opposite and would become argumentative when she drank.

One day there was an addition to the family: a stray Fox Terrier turned up the Wright household. The family named the dog Poochie.

Poochie was a special dog, who, like his owner, was rather adept at winning contests: One Halloween The St. Louis Post Dispatch Newspaper sponsored a photo contest looking for "the best photo of a Halloween Costume." Carol and Jo Ann dressed Poochie like a pig... with a pig mask and a curly tail taped to his stubby tail. His winning photo was displayed with his young owners on the front page of a local paper.

Carol remembers the day her father performed the monstrous act: "One day the Baggets were at our house and Dad was drinking heavily. Dad wanted to show the Baggets what a smart dog we had... Poochie was very nervous when Dad was drinking, so when Dad tried to get him to do a trick we'd taught him, Poochie just stood there, shaking and trembling. Dad grabbed Poochie by a hind leg and repeatedly slammed him against a wall. Poochie would yelp every time he hit the wall and when Dad finally let him go Poochie couldn't walk on his back leg. Though Poochie lived to be 18 years old, he limped on his back leg the rest of his life..."

Incidents like that added to the hardships faced by young Carol. She poured through multiple contest postings around town and competed wherever she could. Her idea to appear as popular cartoon characters earned big points with judges at her grade schools Halloween costume contest.

Dressing up as characters from the *Blondie* comic strip, Carol and her entourage – Jo Ann and Ruth Ann – won first prize. "I believe we won because we dressed up like the characters in a very popular comic strip that people could identify with." Appealing to the taste of her audience was a tactic that Carol would utilize in years to come.

Carol remembers: "After we won, we were told to go on the stage and chose a prize. I chose a baseball bat as my prize. Now I would have my own bat like other kids in the neighborhood. Jo Ann chose a pencil sharpener. She said she picked it because she was tired of never having a sharp pencil at home like the ones at school. Mom would sharpen our pencils with a knife, but she couldn't get a very sharp point on the pencil."

By winning contests and getting her hands on whatever she could, Carol had a knack for making the best of growing up under poor conditions at home. A free baseball bat, a new pencil sharpener – everything added up.

4

Thanks to generous municipal tax dollars allocated to Maplewood School District 187, Carol was able to join the grade school band. Musical instruments, band uniforms, sheet music, and music lessons were all free.

There weren't any organized sports for girls at this time, so Carol had to find other ways to satisfy her competitive spirit. Already excelling in school, she strove to find new arenas to put herself ahead of the pack.

Maplewood Grade School Band was well known for its first place superior ratings at band contests. Carol was assigned to the percussion section of the band....the only girl in that section. Her instructor, Miss Hare, nurtured her budding musical abilities and saw a link between the natures of percussion and dance, at which Carol was adept. Within no time at all, Carol was pinning award medals to the front of her band uniform.

Keeping hold of their finances proved to be a continual worry of the Wright family. After a meager Thanksgiving feast and with the Christmas season fast approaching, money was in short supply for the Wrights.

"When I was six years old, Mom decided to get a job at the Stix Baer & Fuller Department Store in downtown St. Louis to earn Christmas money," recollects Carol, "She was hired as a Christmas wrapper. It was her job to wrap Christmas purchases for the store's customers. Mom worked evenings so Dad could stay home with us kids."

At first, Walter seemed to appreciate this additional quality time with his daughters, but it soon depreciated into another opportunity to belittle and victimize his family. Carol remembers how after an evening of trying to complete a jigsaw puzzle, her frustrated father swept the pieces to the floor, shouting profanities before leaving on another trip to 'cool off.'

"When Mom arrived home from work she was angry he had left us alone," Carol says, "Dad staggered home later, argumentative and cranky. He complained about Mom's job and said her cooking wasn't any good now that she worked. With a sinister look on his face, he went to the refrigerator and dumped all the food that was inside onto the kitchen floor. Then he stumbled off to bed, leaving Mom, Jo Ann, and me to clean up the mess."

This wouldn't be the last time Walter's behavior would become erratic while he was intoxicated. Carol notes: "He had come home another time mad, with that same sinister look on his face. That time he said he didn't like the color of the kitchen floor and painted the tiled floor pink. It took Mom all night to get the paint off the floor."

Trying to please her husband, Wilma quit her job at the department store and took a new position that Walter approved of: a cleaning lady in a local tavern. As her husband frequented that bar, among others, Wilma soon had little escape from her husband's presence. Her nights degenerated into cleaning up after drunks, wiping their spit off the floor.

For Christmas dinner, the Wrights accepted an invitation to the home of Walters Aunt and Uncle in Troy, Illinois. Having recently gotten his hands on an old Chevy Coupe from a co-worker, Walter put the family behind schedule on their trip by stopping on the way home at a bar. His ardiness forced them to travel in dangerous conditions on Christmas Eve, putting them all in mortal danger. Carol remembers that night vividly: "Dad was late getting home ... when he did arrive, it was snowing and he was drinking. Mom didn't want to go and she pleaded with him to wait until the morning. Dad wouldn't hear of it! Fortunately, there wasn't much traffic on the roads that night as we slid from one side of the road to the other..."

The family never made it out of town. As they made their way to the highway, the car slid out of control and hit a telephone pole. On impact, the gearshift slammed into Carol, positioned in the middle of the car seat, knocking her unconscious. When she came to, she was horrified to see her sisters face covered in blood. Jo Ann had slammed right into the windshield, and was injured badly.

Walter was able to get the car running and drove his shaken family to the office of Dr. Curran, a former army doctor known for being rough with his patients. Curran practiced out of his own home in Maplewood Park and was the closest available source of medical care.

Examining Jo Ann's head wound, Curran made the effort to stitch her up but didn't use any anesthetic to numb the pain. "Dad didn't like this and told the doctor he wasn't sewing up my sister's head unless he deadened it first," Carol says, "The doctor and Dad got into a heated argument. The doctor's wife lashed out at Dad, reprimanding him for having endangered his family by driving intoxicated in a blizzard."

Angry at having his folly pointed out, Walter grabbed his still-bleeding daughter and stormed out of the office. At St. Mary's hospital (where Carol was born) Jo Ann's wound was finally stitched up, though doctors warned that she would probably have a small scar when it finally healed.

As the beleaguered family returned home the next morning, the daughters found Christmas presents under the tree waiting for them. In spite of her father's recklessness the night before, Wilma defended her husband's actions at the doctors office.

"Mom told us she was proud that Dad hadn't let Dr. Curran stitch up Jo Ann's head," says Carol, " I thought to myself: *If Dad hadn't come home drinking and insist we go out in a blizzard, the incident wouldn't have happened and Jo Ann would not have needed stitches."*

Although it was hard for her to understand at the time, Carol can now make sense of the way her mother relentlessly stood by her father and explained away his misdeeds. "Mom had a way of twisting things around so they didn't seem so bad. Perhaps this was her way of keeping her sanity, and I think she did love our Dad," she says.

That spring, Walter began 'moonlighting' as a bricklayer with his cousin Everett Jones. The work was hard and the hours long, but Walter began making extra money to support his family. It seemed as if Walter had turned over a new leaf, being too tired after a hard days work to engage in the heavy drinking that he was accustomed to. Within months, the quality of his workmanship was well-known and his skills were in high demand.

Sometimes Carol would accompany Dad on a job site. She remembers the day that put an end to her father's newfound good fortune: "Two union officials came to where Dad and Everett were working. The men said the visit was just a warning, but if he and Everett continued "scabbing", the houses they worked on might be smeared with paint or tar."

Labor Unions feared losing potential work to a non-union tradesman like Walter. Because 'moonlighting' workers provided a cheaper alternative to union members, organized labor turned to intimidation to control the labor market.

Walter went back to his old ways of drinking and hanging out at taverns. The money he'd saved up as a bricklayer was soon gone, and he joined the local Veterans of Foreign Wars hall because drinks were cheaper there. Walter soon became an active member of the VFW and did a lot of work around the Hall. He hadn't been a member very long when Carol heard about a Veteran's Day essay contest that the post was sponsoring. Taking a gamble, she decided to enter the contest.

5

Carol set out to win the essay contest and claim the $25 cash prize. Writing was a new field of competition for her, and she armed herself with the tools she needed for victory.

"I believed then, and still believe today, that if you are going to write about something you must gather as much information regarding the topic as you possibly can to make sure you're informed enough for persuasive logic ... I wasn't familiar with any veteran's organizations or affairs, so I knew I had much to learn."

For a young girl in the era before the internet and home computers, this was easier said than done. Carol decided to consult Commander O.H. Venable of the VFW for advice.

"Commander Venable was a very nice man and he seemed quite flattered that I wanted to enter the contest," Carol remembers, "He explained that Veteran's Day was a day that had been set aside to honor all service men and women who have served for the United States."

As Commander Venable explained the history and meaning of Veterans' Day, Carol gleaned more information, inquiring how many members the VFW hall had and who the oldest member was. Venable pointed her to aging veteran Joe McClusky. Carol decided to base her essay on the experiences of this particular veteran. McClusky lived not far from her grandparents, and Carol knew just where to find him.

"I thought he looked like a really old man, and he was hard of hearing. I talked as loudly as I could, practically shouting to him when I told him I was writing an essay about Veteran's Day and wondered if he would talk to me about some of his war experiences. His eyes lit up, and he said he would be very happy to talk about his military service. I found what he had to say to be most interesting."

Carol found that McClusky had served in the Spanish-American War, and while in Cuba he became very ill; he was 23 years old at the time. Feeling that she'd gleaned enough information from her tiring interviewee, she raced home to write her essay.

"I felt confident this was going to be a most interesting article. I won the essay contest and my essay was displayed on a bulletin board at the VFW post for a long time. Dad was proud and bragged to his veteran friends that his daughter had written the essay."

Carol used the prize money to get new roller skates, shoes and socks, and took away some important lessons from the essay experience.

"I believed then, and still believe today, that people like to read about something that is interesting, not just a collection of facts. I have passed this advice on to my family and it seems to work," she notes.

"Dad spent most of his time at the VFW," says Carol, "When he was home the issue of selling our house became a problem again. He still wanted to sell the house and build a brick home. Mom didn't want to sell...she wanted to stay put and refused to sign any papers, even after Dad put a for sale sign in the front yard."

Carol recalls when the dispute grew more serious: "One hot summer night he came home in a most lousy mood, growling: "If I can't sell this ... house then you're not sleeping in it.' He pushed Mom, Jo Ann, and I out into the night, locking the storm door behind us...We walked to Maplewood Grade School and sat down on baseball bleacher seats. It was the middle of the night, but light out because there was a full moon. Mom sat on a bleacher seat and cried. We ended up sleeping overnight in a sports equipment shed."

The next day, Walter acted as if nothing had happened, but Wilma did agree to sell the house. Carol muses that her father seemed to have a split personality brought out by intoxication.

"I sometimes wondered if Dad couldn't remember half the stuff he did, because when he was sober he would be a real nice guy. He and I would go fishing, fly a kite, or walk along the railroad tracks searching for wild turnip greens."

The neighbors noticed his alcoholism, the consensus being: "Walter is such a nice man sober, but when he gets liquored up, watch out!" While they said it with a shrug of the shoulders, the Wright girls experienced it day and night.

The house sold quickly. Walter and Wilma paid their mortgage off and bought an undeveloped lot on the 'good side' of Maplewood. Paul Baggett offered to rent the family three upstairs rooms of his house ... a bedroom, a kitchen, and a bathroom. The Baggetts lived just outside Maplewood in a small village, Walnut Grove, and this was where the Wrights would stay as Walter built their new house.

However, Walter was slow to get the job underway, and took to his old habits of drinking with Paul and Dotty Baggett on the weekends. During the week, he worked at the Aluminum Ore Plant, Paul worked in the train yards at Union Station in St. Louis, and Mom worked part-time cleaning Jules Tavern. Dotty didn't work outside the home but she'd often be gone most of the day at a bar. Carol recalls: "She was quite proficient at cooking a meal real quick in a pressure cooker so Paul wouldn't know she had been gone most of the day."

"We still had Poochie when we moved to Baggett's house, but he wasn't the only animal living there," says Carol, "We had an adopted gray and white female cat that we named Fluffy, and the Baggett family had a beautiful orange cat ...

Everything was fine with the animals until Fluffy had two kittens. This very much irritated Paul and Dad. One day, Paul and Dad decided they'd get rid of all those cats. Both men, as usual, were drunk. Paul grabbed the orange cat and tightly clasped his hands around the cat's neck..."

The terrified cat jerked and squirmed as Paul squeezed the cat's throat tighter and tighter. The young girls were hysterical, and pulled frantically on their father's arms, but Paul was too strong. He strangled the cat to death in front of his two children.

Walter decided against such brutality and opted to drop Fluffy and her litter along the side of a nearby highway before reconsidering and going back to collect the cats.

The next day Wilma commented how good it was that Dad didn't kill Fluffy or her kittens and how, after he dumped them along the highway, he went back and got them. Carol was not so quick to forget, however:

"I thought to myself, *Mom's doing it again, twisting things so they didn't appear so bad...*"

The surprises at the Baggett house kept on coming, and became even more ghastly. Carol recalls how her father even brought physical harm on his friends and landlords, the Baggetts:

"Once when Paul, Dotty, and Dad were drunk, Dotty was heating oil in a skillet on her kitchen stove... Dotty fell on the floor in a corner of her kitchen, and urinated on herself. Dad grabbed the skillet and flung the oil at Dotty, but he missed. Instead, the hot oil went on Paul's face and across Mom's back. Paul's eyes were spared, but blisters soon formed on his face and on Mom's back. As hard as it was to believe, Paul didn't get mad at Dad."

When school started, the Wright girls transferred to a new school, located on Route 3 across from Phillips Oil Refinery. The place, as Carol put it, "didn't have a very scenic view."

One day, Carol's new teacher announced that she was having a poetry contest, and that her students could write about anything, or anyone, we wanted. It didn't take Carol long to decide on the topic of her poem: "I would write about Paul Revere because I had just written a report about him in history class. This would be a subject I would know something about."

As she tried her hand at poetry, Carol couldn't get over how easily the words came to her: "It was as if someone else was guiding my pencil and writing the poem for me. I've read this is what professional writers refer to as 'being in the zone'."

Unfortunately, her final piece would be looked upon with suspicion from her teachers who were unfamiliar with Carol's talent and intelligence. Soon after submitting her poem, Carol was summoned to the Principals office to explain herself.

"Did you copy your poem, Caroleen?" the Principal asked.
Carol responded that she hadn't.
"Did someone write your poem for you?" her teacher, Mrs. Black, asked.
Again she said no.

The Principal and Mrs. Black didn't believe Carol, who was punished for "lying" and consigned away to detention. "I was crushed," Carol says. "The poet award went to another student and for the rest of the year I knew that Mrs. Black didn't like or trust me."

This was the one contest that Carol would not win.

6

Not all of Carol's childhood memories were plagued by alcoholism and family infighting. She recalls fond memories of her hometown of Maplewood where her old grade school still stands, a relic of a bygone age.

Maplewood Park was a small working class community in Illinois, before it was Annxed into the nearby township of Cahokia.

"Most of the men who lived in Maplewood Park worked at nearby industries in Sauget, Il, and St. Louis," Carol says, "Some women worked outside the home, but most were traditional housewives. If you strolled down any street on a Monday you would see row after row of clothing hanging on clothes lines... Most of these garments were 100% cotton, so Tuesdays were set aside for ironing and the task usually took all day, depending on the size of the family."

Carol remembers how what could now be accomplished in a day, or even in hours, once made up the routine for an entire week: "Many of the women baked on Wednesdays, and sewed on Thursdays. Fridays were "clean the house" day and Saturdays a day for shopping. We didn't attend church, but for those who did, Sunday was a day for worshiping," she says.

"My Grandpa and Grandma Gray moved to Maplewood in 1922 and built a home there, "says Carol, "He was lucky he had employment during The Great Depression, and afterward. He was a carpenter and was hired to work in the maintenance department for the Maplewood School District. His family had it easier than many of the other families living in Maplewood Park during the 1930's, as the national unemployment rate skyrocketed to 80%.

The War years were hard on civilians at home as well as soldiers, with rationing laws making their way to the Midwest and affecting every family.

"While Dad was away serving in the army," Carol says, "We had to contend with the rationing of certain goods such as meat, sugar, and butter because all these commodities were needed for soldiers. Instead of butter we had Oleo, a sort of margarine that was white, but came with a packet of coloring so it could be colored to look more like butter. Mom would let me blend the Oleo and coloring together."

The rationing extended to all walks of life, making things even tougher for a family just trying to get by. In spite of it all, Wilma tried her best to maintain a façade of normalcy.

"Nylons were hard to come by," says Carol, "So Mom would draw a black line down the back of her leg to make it appear as if she was wearing nylons."

During the War while her father was away, Carol spent a lot of time at her grand parent's house, helping her grandfather in the garden and generally making herself at home.

"He had two cherry trees along the side of his driveway and I would help him pick ripe cherries from the trees. Sometimes I would climb almost to the top of the trees to get the juicy fruit. He'd pay me 5 cents for every galvanized bucket of cherries that I picked," she recalls fondly. Her efforts did not go without further reward: "Grand-Ma made delicious cherry pies from the fruit, and cAnnd the rest of the cherries to use later to bake more pies and treats."

Eggs were generally supplied from backyard chicken-coops, but there came a time when Carol's grandparents got rid of the coop and had their eggs delivered by an "egg man".

"The "egg man" was a weird looking fellow because of his

terrible dentures. His teeth looked like the yellow corn kernels on a corn cob. What made him look uglier was that he was always smiling. If he would have kept his mouth shut he wouldn't have looked so bad," says Carol.

Carol remembers her grandfather well: "He liked nothing better than to sit and drink hot coffee, smoke a Camel cigarette, and listen to a St. Louis Cardinals Baseball game on the radio announced by Harry Carrey."

Many of the homes in Maplewood Park had a small "mother-in-law" house at the back of the property away from the main house. In the era before retirement homes and with a stronger sense of family duty, this was how people cared for aging parents. "It was a good arrangement for little children", notes Carol, "Because their grandparents were only a stone's throw away."

A common sight in Maplewood was the noisy propeller airplanes that flew low over the roof tops of houses. The pilots were students from nearby Parks Air College, and they would fly so low they'd wave to a young Carol on the ground from their open cockpits. However, accidents did occasionally happen, often with tragic results.

Carol remembers once incident particularly well: "One day when Grand-Pa and I were working in his garden a propeller airplane crashed in a field at the end of our neighborhood... As soon as my grandpa heard the crash he immediately grabbed his shovel and we jumped into his car and drove to the crash site. Other people were already there, trying to extinguish a fire in the airplane with their shovels and dirt. Grand-Pa told me to stay put and he ran to help fight the fire."

His heroism, however timely, was too late to save the downed pilots. "The two men trapped in the airplane were burned alive and I can still remember their high shrill screams," Carol recalls.

In a small town, the local movie theater often finds itself near the center of social life. For a young Carol, Maplewood Theater was to become the place where her contest-winning streak would hit the big-time as she won her very first sweepstakes.

"As always, I was on the alert for a contest," Carol remembers, "When I learned that there was going to be a sweepstakes drawing at the theater during intermission, I couldn't resist, even though I had never won a sweepstakes."

The sweepstakes was different from the various contests Carol had won because it was a random drawing., and not the talent-based contests she'd done so well in before. This time there was no one to impress, no one to judge, and seemingly little she could do to stand out from the crowd of others entering the draw.

"Though it was a random drawing, I felt that I should still do something," she says, "I decided to fan fold my entry, hoping this would enhance my chance of winning by giving my entry body and perhaps a different feel to the person conducting the drawing. It worked! I was thrilled when I heard my name called and it was announced that I I was one of the five lucky people to win a $20 bill."

This wouldn't be the last time Carol managed to win a random draw – including one with even higher stakes.

"I have won several sweepstakes...the biggest prizes being a LHS Chrysler car – I submitted the entry in Don's name – and a $10,000 shopping spree at an upscale mall in St. Louis," she says. "I have come up with more creative, innovative techniques to enhance my chances for winning sweepstakes."

7

Growing up in Maplewood also presented its share of challenges. Carol's younger sister Jo Ann was also victimized by her father, sometimes unintentionally. Assuming that his daughter Jo Ann also had a talent for winning contests, Walter nominated her in a VFW beauty pageant to be crowned 'Queen of the Post'.

Carol recalls that "Jo Ann was shy, easily intimidated, and emotionally beaten down by our father. She didn't seek, or enjoy being in the limelight, and had no desire to be the center of attention. My poor sister, however, had no choice but to comply with Dad's wishes and be a candidate."

The Queen would be chosen, based on the number of raffle tickets the candidates and her family sold. Walter paraded his young daughters to the several local bars he haunted, and they managed to sell all the raffle tickets. Like it or not, Jo Ann was now Queen of VFW Post number 1699.

One of her first duties as Queen was to ride in the Maplewood Homecoming Parade and wave to spectators from the seat of a convertible car. Carol recalls her sister not particularly enjoying her moment in the sun, "I don't think she felt like a beauty, although she certainly was one. After the parade she had to walk the grounds at the Homecoming Picnic and mingle with the people there. Jo Ann told me later that she hated the whole affair."

Despite this, Carol managed to take away another lesson that would benefit her in the years to come: "If you want to sell raffle tickets, or anything else for that matter, go to a tavern or bowling alley where there are a lot of people drinking. Drunks will buy anything!"

8

The arrival of summer 1951 found the Wrights still marooned at the Baggetts' home, with Walter still unwilling to begin work on a new house. Instead, he spent most of his spare time in bars or going fishing. When school let out, Walter announced a week-long fishing trip on Horseshoe Lake in Southern Illinois ... it would be just the Wright family.

"It was a wonderful week," says Carol, "Dad didn't drink anything alcoholic all the time we were there. We stayed in a rustic, but comfortable little cabin near the lake, and there was a rowboat that was included with the cabin."

"During the day Dad and I would fish from the boat," Carol remembers, "In the evening Dad cleaned the fish and Mom cooked the perch, bluegill, and catfish. The week at the lake was so idyllic that I hated to go home."

Walter must have shared her feelings, because upon their return to the Baggett home, he announced that he'd rented the cabin again for the Fourth of July weekend. And since Walter had a large sedan, he would drive the two families on the trip.

"Everyone was in good spirits when we left," Carol says, "We stopped at almost every tavern along the way and by early afternoon Dad, Paul, and Dotty were getting intoxicated."

Somewhere along the way, Walter and Dotty started arguing. "She didn't like his driving and complained that he was driving too fast," Carol says, "The more she complained about his driving, the faster he'd drive. I felt certain the police would pull Dad over. We started down a long steep hill and at the bottom there was a bridge that spAnnd a river. As we went down the hill the car quickly picked up speed. Dotty was screaming (profanities), and Mom was begging Dad to slow down. Paul sat there in a stupor. Jane, Ann, Jo Ann, and I were crying. I could see the speedometer from the backseat of the car and it showed we were going almost 90 miles per hour. I felt certain Dad would not make it across the narrow bridge at the bottom of the hill. I knew we were all going to die."

Miraculously, Walter guided the car safely over the bridge, and once on the other side, slammed on the brakes. The car almost flipped when the tires skidded in the loose gravel.

As soon as the certainty of danger passed, Dotty leapt from the vehicle, shouting that she was going to walk back to Maplewood. Only the tearful cries of her daughters kept her from abandoning the group, and Paul's grumbled command to 'keep her mouth shut' avoided any further confrontation. Other than this close brush with disaster, the trip to the lake was a great success. Walter and Paul developed such a fondness for fishing that they'd take their daughters out with them nearly every weekend. While all this fishing prevented Walter from getting started on building his family a new home, it also stood in the way of Carol winning more contests.

"The weekends when we were home I'd scour the Sunday newspapers, looking for contests," she says, "One Sunday I read that a local Sportsman club was sponsoring a fishing contest. The ad stated there would be a prize for the biggest fish caught, and a prize for who caught the most fish. I told Dad about the contest and suggested that we enter. He didn't want to, but did offer to mix up a batch of dough bait for me to use. He claimed his bait was special because of a secret ingredient ... honey. 'You can catch more flies with honey than vinegar,' he said, 'and this is also true of fish.'"

Carol came in second place in the contest and won a new fishing pole and line, but the modern equipment didn't suit her style, and she soon took back to fishing with her old bamboo pole. Even still, she took an important lesson away from that competition, and from her father.

"Decades later when I would enter cooking contests I remembered how my Dad used a secret ingredient for his bait," she says, "Whenever it was possible I would add an unusual ingredient to make my recipe better and unusual Once I baked a pickle cake for a contest and my cake was the talk of the event."

Changes were on the horizon for the Baggetts, and by consequence for the Wrights as well. Dotty became pregnant and for the Wrights, this turned out to not be very good news.

"Dotty had a baby boy that summer," Carol remembers, "Dad was extremely jealous that Paul had a son, and he didn't. Dad wanted a baby, but Mom refused. One night in a fit of anger he threw their mattress down the stairs that led up to our rooms at the Baggetts' house."

The Baggetts had had enough of Walter's outbursts and evicted the family. The Wrights then rented a small four-room house in the Harvest Acres subdivision in Maplewood.

Wilma quit her cleaning job at the tavern and went looking for a better job, seeking employment at the Aluminum Ore Plant where Dad worked. She applied for a job as a secretary, but found that she hadn't retained her typing skills, losing her speed. Carol remembers how her father used this as yet another opportunity to berate her mother: "Dad ridiculed her for flunking the test, and threw it up to her that she was a high school graduate and couldn't pass a simple typing test."

However, Wilma found a steady job at the corporate offices of the Edison Brothers Shoe Company in St. Louis as a shoe distributor. It was a steady job that she would keep for thirty-two years, though she would have to make a long commute to get to work. While this helped the Wright's money situation, there were even more clouds on the horizon.

"Dad's drinking was escalating," says Carol, "On Fridays

he'd get his pay check early and leave work so he could start drinking at noon. He'd come home intoxicated and take Mom, Jo Ann, and I to places a child should never go to."

"Once he took us to a burlesque show in Old Cahokia. Jo Ann and I were embarrassed by the naked ladies on the stage, so we put our hands over our eyes. A customer at the joint came over to my parents and berated them for having young children there. I think Dad got some kind of obscene pleasure by taking us to such places," Carol says.

The more Walter went out to drink, the more reckless and violent he became. After coming home in a typically bad mood, he got into an argument with his wife and attacked her, beating her within sight of his terrified daughters. "The look in his eye made me terrified that he would kill my mother," says Carol.

"There was a nice young couple that lived in the neighborhood two houses down from our house. They liked Jo Ann and I ... we often went over to their house to play with their puppies. I ran to their house and knocked on the door. When the man opened the door I pleaded with him to come with me and help save Mom. I could still hear Mom screaming as I stood there."

"I don't want to get involved," the man said, and slowly closed the door.

"I ran back home. Dad was no longer brutalizing Mom and had gone into their bedroom to lay down. Mom's nose was bleeding, her face was awash with tears, and her hair was a mess. I helped her get up and gave her a cold wash cloth to put on her face. Jo Ann was cowering in a corner of the living room."

At her young age, Carol couldn't understand the social politics that kept an upstanding young man from coming to help when he heard the screams caused by domestic violence.

She knew, however, that neither she nor her sister would ever visit the young couple again.

Walter's violence directed itself also towards Poochie.

"Dad came home one night drinking. When he opened the door Poochie ran out. Dad called him, but Poochie paid him no mind," Carol remembers.

"I'm going to shoot that damn dog," Dad threatened.

He went and got his old shot gun and started for the door. Carol knew he would shoot her beloved dog, and so ran out of the house ahead of her raging father.

"You go near that damn dog, and I'll shoot you too," he shouted.

Carol grabbed Poochie and ran as fast as she could across the street and away from her family's house. Her efforts were sabotaged by a full moon, making it easy for her father to track her movements. With his white hair, Poochie was an easy target in the bright moonlight.

"I heard Dad's car engine start. Holding Poochie tightly, I crouched down behind a row of bushes in a neighbor's yard. Dad's car passed by, and as he went by I could see the barrel of his gun resting on the rolled down window sill of the driver's side of the car," says Carol, "Cautiously I crept out of our hiding place and we ran through more yards trying to get out of the neighborhood.

Her father's pursuit became even more sinister and Carol began to fear for her life. It was as if she was chased not by her father, but a deranged lunatic.

"I could see Dad's car slowly driving up and down the streets...his was the only vehicle on the road that time of night," she says, "It was a cat and mouse game, with Dad being the cat and Poochie and I the mice. The night was surreal...like I was in a movie, or worst yet, a horrific nightmare."

Carol decided to find Poochie a sanctuary in the nearby home of her maternal grandparents, who hadn't seen Carol in years as they didn't like Walter. Deciding that she didn't have very many options, Carol elected to give it a try.

"I knocked on the door to wake them up. When they saw me standing there at the front door...their faces were in shock," she recalls, "When I told them what had happened, they were even more shocked. Grand-Pa quickly turned off the lights so Dad wouldn't know I was there. That was a smart move, because shortly thereafter, Dad drove by their house."

Carol's grandparents went next-door to use Grandma Gray's brother's telephone. Not surprisingly, Walter had a reputation in the community for boozing, and the phrase 'Walter Wright is after our granddaughter with a gun', roused neighbors and the police to action.

"The police went to our house in Harvest Acres to see if Mom and Jo Ann were alright," says Carol, "They brought them to Grandpa and Grandma's house. Then they went looking for Dad, and when they found him he didn't have a gun. He denied threatening to shoot me and the police let him go. Mom signed a peace bond against Dad which cost her $10, but Dad didn't have to pay anything, even though the whole incident had been his fault."

The badly shaken Wright girls and their mother stayed with the girls' grandparents that night, and later moved in with them. Walter sunk deeper into alcoholism and eventually resumed his friendship with Paul and Dotty Baggett. This friendship had pulled him down into alcoholism and violence before, but this time it would end in death.

"Late one night a policeman came to my grandparent's house, telling Mom that Dad had been in an automobile accident. He had been bar-hopping with the Baggett's, and while they were taking Dad home, their car was hit by a freight train," Carol says.

Dotty had been driving with her three young children in the front seat with her while the men rode in back. The train impacted with the car on the side where Paul Baggett sat. He died en route to the hospital. In a morbidly ironic turn, Dotty's father was revealed to be the engineer driving the train. Walter wasn't seriously hurt and was found near the accident site with only minor cuts and bruises.

"Paul's funeral was sad. Jane wouldn't talk to me at the funeral home, or after that. Whenever I saw her she wouldn't have anything to do with me," Carol says, "Dad was traumatized... he looked pale and gaunt. He begged Mom to return home. He sounded sincere ... promised that if she would come home he'd start working on the new house."

Because Wilma hated living with her parents and felt sorry for the distraught Walter, she moved back into the small rental home once again.

Carol and her sister didn't like living with their grandparents either. To cope with the boredom of not having any toys or being allowed to bring friends over, she turned to competition and contests as a way to pass the time.

"At the time, *The East St. Louis Journal Newspaper* was running a crosswords puzzle contest," she says, "The puzzles were difficult to solve because more than one word would often fit in the spaces. We would collect copies of the paper from our neighbors. In the rules there wasn't any stipulation that a person could only enter the contest once, so Grand-Pa and I would send in several different completed puzzles."

Though they won on several occasions, working on the crosswords passed the time and taught Carol another crucial lesson about contest entry: "I always read the rules of a contest or sweepstakes, and if the rules state that it is okay to enter more than once, that is what I will do. This increases the odds of winning, and when I enter a contest or sweepstakes, I enter with a positive attitude... I expect to win!"

9

That fall, a high school was built for the teenagers of the newly incorporated village of Cahokia, of which Maplewood was now a part. Cahokia Commonfields High School was a large, modern building that gathered up many students who hadn't seen each other in years. Carol would attend this institution for her junior high school years. Unfortunately for Carol, she found herself alone and with few friends, unfamiliar with the system of cliques that define high school.

"At a special assembly to choose cheerleaders I sat down next to a skinny, blond girl named Mary Simmons. We had been classmates at Maplewood Grade School when I attended the school" Carol remembers, "Mary -bless her heart- invited me to join her group of friends. It was big relief to finally have friends to hang out with." Mary remains Carol's good friend to this day.

Though she would later win a spot on the cheerleading squad as a substitute, Carol directed most of my energy toward school studies and playing the drums in the junior high band. Her enthusiasm for school didn't always help her win the affections of her peers.

Things at home seemed to have finally stabilized as well. As fall segued into winter, Walter and Wilma maintained steady jobs at the shoe company and aluminum ore plant, respectively. Walter had managed to refrain from heavy drinking, and was finally planning to start construction on the new family home. The quick arrival of winter made laying a foundation impossible, and plans to build were put on hold yet again. It was an uneventful winter until young Jo Ann woke up one morning and found that she couldn't move.

"She had to crawl to get to the living room," remembers Carol, "Jo Ann was diagnosed as having hepatitis. The doctor informed Mom that Jo Ann had a light case and said he could treat her at home."

Although Jo Ann was left home alone during her sickness due to her mothers obligations at work, Jo Ann relentlessly followed doctors' orders and stayed on top of her school work, making a full recovery in a few weeks.

When winter gave way to spring, Walter, at long last, began construction on the new house with an eager spirit. Even Wilma contributed to the effort, helping lay the stones of the house foundation.

Despite the calm atmosphere that had fallen upon her family, Carol still felt a sense of unease when opportunities came to take a break and get away from the house for a while, like when some of Wilma's old friends from high school offered to take the girls to their farm for a week.

"I was scared about leaving mom alone with dad for a week," Carol remembers, "He could kill her while I was gone. Part of me thought that if I was there I could do something to stop it."

10

That spring, Walter's seldom-seen, and even less heard-from father came to visit. There had been bitterness for a long from Walter towards his dad, not only because of his lack of affection during Walter's childhood, but also because he never made much effort to keep in touch with his son after he went out into the world. Carol vividly recalls when her estranged grandfather and Dad's sister, Aunt Francis, came to call:

"Grand-Pa Wright was a tall, gaunt man. He brought a big old trunk with him that contained their clothes, some keepsakes, and a Bible. Francis watched over that trunk diligently, and became quite agitated if anyone got near it."

Walter's sister, Francis, suffered from cerebral palsy, limiting her movements and making her speech hard to understand. Although Wilma diligently waited on her father in-law hand and foot, Walter mostly ignored his father. The elder Wright returned the sentiment by essentially ignoring his grandchildren during his stay. Despite her grandfather's attitude, Carol does remember one positive comment he made to his son at this time:

"You've got yourself a good woman there, son. You should treat her better."

The elder Wright slept during most of his stay, and often complained that he was suffering from severe headaches. When his family took him to a hospital, Carol learned that her grandfather had an inoperable brain tumor and would not be long for the world. She remembers her grandfather's last days:

"His pain was excruciating, so much so that he would howl in pain. Most of the time he didn't know what he was doing...he ripped off his clothes and ran nude down a corridor at the hospital. He didn't recognize Dad, Mom, or his brother, Uncle Jim Wright. He became so violent that he threw things and tried to strike the nurses. An orderly restrained him in bed with a wide leather strap, but Grand-Pa was so strong he broke the straps. The next day, he was dead."

If Walter's relationship with his father had lacked warmth, the funeral was an affair as cold as could be imagined. His father's will stipulated that his mistress would be the beneficiary of the estate, so Walter and his brothers were liable for all funeral expenses. His brothers refused to pay their share, so Walter had to dig deep to pay for the funeral of a man who had never shown him much affection. Grandpa Wright was buried at the family plot of his brother Jim Wright, in an unmarked grave at Troy IL.

"After Grand-Pa Wright's funeral Francis didn't have anywhere to go, so Dad and Mom brought her home with us," says Carol, "Jo Ann and I didn't know what to think of her...we'd never been around handicapped person before. She was an asset to the family, not a liability. Accustomed to not having much, Francis never complained or asked for anything. She was an excellent cook and had supper on the table when Mom came home from work, and kept the house clean."

Although the addition of Francis to her household made some things easier for Wilma, a visiting social worker became the first to express unease at the arrangement and recommended that their handicapped relative be placed in an institution. The Wrights didn't take much notice of these suggestions. The death of his father was another setback for Walter's home building project, and he hit the bottle hard.

"Some of his antics could be downright comical unless you lived with him," says Carol, "One time he came home bald. A man at a tavern had dared Dad to let them shave his head. When he awoke the next day he was shocked to see himself in a mirror."

Despite incidents like that, Walters alcoholism was steadily taking a turn from buffoonery to sadism. Carol remembers the escalation well, and how soon it became directed against her and her sister:

"He bullied Mom and Jo Ann more then me. He'd tell Jo Ann to get him some ice cubes out of the freezer in the refrigerator, but when she'd go to the refrigerator to get the ice cubes, he would slam the door on her arm. I wasn't as scared as (my mother and sister). Once he called me "snake eyes" after I stood up to him and stared him down."

Even the helpless Francis became a recipient of abuse. On one occasion, he returned home drunk and forced the entire household into his car, speeding towards the nearby township of Dupo, before pulling to the side of the highway.

"He stopped the car and told Mom, Jo Ann, and I to get out," says Carol, "I knew we had a long walk home Dad peeled out with Francis in the front seat, and she was crying."

Wilma left her husband again and moved back in with her parents, but first had to make arrangements for someone in the family to come collect Francis. Walter's brother James begrudgingly took on the responsibility. Carol would later find out that Francis would be kept in the basement James' home before she was rescued by the authorities and sent to a group home. Carol and her sister never saw their aunt Francis again.

In time, Walter convinced his wife to give him yet another chance. His plan was to move the family into the half-completed basement of their new home with the goal of saving rent money. Before this could happen, however, Walter got himself into yet another calamity. As he drove back from a local tavern, he crashed his car into a telephone pole near Carol's new high school, causing a major blackout in town.

11

Walter suffered a severe injury in the accident and lost part of his eyelid, requiring plastic surgery to correct the damage. Although his operation was paid for by the families insurance, their one means of transportation was now a smoking ruin. "We had to walk to the nearest store, Dillon's Confectionery, for groceries," says Carol, "The owners were very nice and gave Mom credit when she needed it. Thanks to them, we didn't go hungry if money was tight."

Walter still spent the majority of his earning out drinking, making money scarce. "Bill collectors would come to our house to demand payment," says Carol, "It was my job to get rid of them, even if my parents were home. One day a bill collector didn't believe me when I told him that my parents weren't home."

"And just where are your folks?" He asked.
Thinking fast, Carol answered,
"They are at my Aunt Sinky Linky's house," Carol answered, having no idea where that name came from.
"And where does this Aunt live?" he quizzed.
"On Mildred Avenue," she lied.
Shaking his head, the bill collector left, but Carol knew she wouldn't be able to stave off the inevitable forever.

By now, the family was barely getting by on Wilma's salary, a meager $45 dollars per week, forcing Carol and her sister to look for ways to make extra money: "We'd collect empty glass soda, beer, and milk bottles and would receive anywhere from 2 cents to 5 cents per bottle. If we were at a bar with Dad we would look for coins on the tavern's floor or in the parking lot. Occasionally I would get a babysitting job, and if the people were going to be out late, I would stay the night."

Once Walter made the basement at the new house habitable, he moved his family in. He and his wife worked extremely hard building the house, putting in time towards its construction even after working a full work day. Walter had a reputation as a quick and able bricklayer, and work commenced smoothly and the family worked as a team to accomplish their goal. Unfortunately, Carol remembers an incident that would lead to Wilma taking the children and leaving her husband yet again.

"One hot Saturday Dad told Mom he was going to go to Wilson's Tavern and get a cold beer to cool off," she says, "He told her to keep mixing the mortar every so often so it wouldn't solidify. He said he would only be gone for about an hour."

"Mom had her hands full," Carol recalls, "One hour went by...two hours....four hours and Dad wasn't back...Mom was exhausted from keeping the mortar mixed. She walked down to the Tavern. When she went in she saw Dad sitting at the bar, intoxicated. She asked the proprietor of the place not to serve Dad anymore liquor... explaining that she needed him at home. She told how she had been mixing mortar all day to keep it from sitting...the man listened to her patiently, then grabbed a bottle of whiskey from a shelf behind the bar and poured Dad a shot. Everyone in the tavern laughed, and Mom was humiliated."

Wilma took her daughters and went to live in St. Louis, renting a hotel room that summer. They shared a bathroom with the entire floor and all three slept in the same bed. Outside, bright neon advertisements made sleeping even more difficult. During this time, Carol remembers her mother looking sad and worried, even though she was close enough to her place of employment that she could walk to work.

"Mom would lay on the bed and stare at the ceiling for hours," says Carol, "We didn't have any toys or games to play with, so downtown St. Louis became our playground. We would go to department stores and ride the elevators and escalators. We would go to the toy department and look at the toys there. We were always hungry."

Wilma's parents didn't know their daughter was staying in St. Louis. When they found out, they called her at work and convinced her to move back in with them. School was due to start in the fall, and it would be better for the children, so they said. Wilma took the opportunity to face her demons, and told Walter that she was leaving him…this time for good. Walter signed their property deed over to her and she sold the half-constructed house to a friend of her fathers. It was finished in no time, and the family never had their "dream house."

"Mom didn't get much money from the sale of the house," says Carol, "Grandpa advised her to buy a run down duplex on not far from their house. He told her the duplex would provide her with income after she rented out the other side of the house. He promised to help fix the place up – it was a dump."

When school started in the fall, Carol was a freshman, truly a part of her high school. Understandably, she wanted a yearbook to keep track of the memories she made at this time, but family funds were in very short supply. The school needed money to order the yearbooks near the start of the year, so if she wanted to get her hands on one, she needed to think fast!

"It just so happened I saw an announcement on the bulletin board at school about an essay contest that was being sponsored by the St. .Clair County Tuberculosis Association," she says, "The announcement said that one student from each area high school would be chosen and would receive $10. The announcement went on to say that the student who won overall from all the schools would receive $25. I saw this as my way to get the money I needed so I could order my yearbook."

All Carol had to do was write an exceptional essay,

something she'd had experience with in the past. Like her earlier essay for the Veterans association, she didn't know much about the subject matter, so she resolved to do some research and learn more about the terrible disease; tuberculosis.

"Tuberculosis did have my interest because my Dad's mother, had died from the disease shortly after giving birth to the twins," she remembers, "After I gathered the material I needed to write my essay I worked on a catchy opening sentence–very important in essay writing."

Her opening paragraph read:
"There it is. Where? On the doorknob, in the sink, on the wall, or in the air, the tuberculosis germ, tubercle bacillus lingers ready to strike its next victim. The defeat of this unwanted guest, however, is left to the people."

Her essay went on to explain how the wrong kind of foods, not enough rest, worry, fear, sickness, all lower the body's resistance. She was the essay winner for my school and won the $10. Then my essay was selected from seventeen area high schools as the best essay, granting a victorious Carol the additional $25.

Once again, Carol found a way to accomplish her goals through her own ingenuity. Ironically, when the T.B. association came to test students before they started schools, she hid in the bathroom.

"I had a terrible phobia of needles, even fainted when I had to be inoculated (to start school), I didn't get test – me, of all people, the T.B. essay contest winner!"

12

The times were changing in Cahokia. In her sophomore year, the high school was integrated...blacks were bussed in to learn alongside their white peers. "I felt sorry for the new students," says Carol, "but was helpless to do anything for them. I was having a difficult time myself, trying to fit in."

Carol remembers how white students and teachers alike harassed the black students. "Miss Huffman, my English teacher, took a special delight in making the new students stand at the front of the class and pronounce specific words she would give them," she says, "If they didn't say a word (without an accent), Miss Huffman would mock and humiliate them. I spoke with a slight southern accent and feared Miss Huffman might call me to the front of the class to pronounce her words and make fun of and humiliate me."

Carol was comfortable around black people and it dismayed her to see human beings treated in such a derogatory way. Unlike many of her classmates, she'd lived near and known the segregated blacks in her community all her life. Even Walter, a true southern man, had no dislike of black people. They were his co-workers, and often found themselves in the same boat, dealing with problems that affected working black and white families alike.

Though she didn't go to her school prom that year, Carol did serve on its decorating committee. The theme was "One Night in Paris"...little did Carol know that one day she and her daughter would experience the "City of Lights" firsthand.

As the school year passed, Carol grew into a young woman, outgrowing the few clothes and dresses she had. When the year finished, she needed new clothes badly, and knew she would have to start working to pay for them. "I caught a bus and went to St. Louis where I applied for a job at Neisner's

Dime Store," she says, "I was under age (14), had no job skills, and didn't have a clue as to the proper attire to wear for a job interview. Still I was hired as a waitress and was provided pink outfits to wear. This was good because now I wouldn't have to buy clothes for my job and could save money for school clothes."

Carol worked at Neisner's Dime Store all summer and used most of her earnings to buy school clothes. Since girls weren't allowed to wear pants to school, she purchased skirts and tops. Carol shared her clothes with the growing Jo Ann.

In her junior year, Carol joined her school paper and was selected to be the editor, but found the work to be more than she could handle. She passed on the duties to a friend and took on her role as a reporter. As a reporter, she had carte blanch and got to write whatever she wanted. She was also the cartoonist, created crossword puzzles about students and school events, and was yearbook editor. Carol still played the drums in the high school band, though she was saddened that nobody from her family came to any band concerts. She later joined an all girls combo that specialized in jazz music. She didn't feel singled out by this lack of attention: Jo Ann played the saxophone in the junior high band and was given the brush off by her family as well.

"My junior year I attended the Prom," she remembers, "Mom managed to buy me a pretty pink prom dress. My date was Winston Stuart. The prom was a magical night. After the dance we went to the Kiel Auditorium in St. Louis to see "Bill Haley and The Comets." I sat down, not knowing I was supposed to pull the seat down. I felt foolish, engulfed in my fluffy soft pink organza dress on the floor. Like many of my friends I started smoking. A pack of cigarettes cost 25 cents, the same price as a school lunch. I used the lunch money Mom gave me to buy my cigarettes," Carol admits, "I'd wait until I got home from school to eat, and I was famished because I never ate breakfast. My sister started smoking at about the same time I did, even though she was three years younger."

Life was peaceful until Wilma allowed Walter to move into the duplex with his family. He had been fired from his job at Aluminum Ore Plant for taking too many days off work, but soon got employment as a brick layer for a local contractor. Old habits die hard, and Walter still regularly cashed his paychecks at the local tavern. During this time, Walter became increasingly violent and ill-tempered. He was the unquestioned master of his household, and his reach over each family member became more dominating every day.

Around this time, Carol believes she witnessed the de-facto *rape* of her mother by Walter: "One particular Friday night Dad came home drunk from the bar earlier than usual at about 7 p.m. and he was in a particularly fowl mood. When he'd come home in a mood like this it usually meant he'd had an disagreement with someone at the tavern, but rather than attack the person he'd disagreed with, he would come home and take his agitation out on Mom, my sister, and I."

"As soon as he got home that night he started arguing with Mom...slapping and pushing her. He forced my sister and I to sit in chairs at the kitchen table and listen to him rant and rave. Mom was very frightened and was crying because no matter how she answered him, it was always the wrong answer. Finally he grabbed her by the hair and pushed her into the bedroom, shouting at Jo Ann and me to go to our room and get into bed and turn out the lights. Jo Ann and I went to our room and turned out the lights, but we certainly didn't go to sleep. We could hear everything that was going on in our parent's bedroom...the grunting sounds and Mom crying and saying, "Don't Walter...please don't. You're hurting me."

Carol was fourteen and old enough to know what was going on, yet there wasn't anything she could do except stay in her room, and pray that her mother would be alright. "After what seemed like a long time, there was silence and then the rhythmic sound of Dad's snoring," she says. "I heard Mom go to the bathroom and vomit. I felt sick myself, and thought I might vomit too. The next morning when Dad got up he acted as if nothing had happened the night before...but my sister and I never forgot, and we never will."

13

School let out for the summer, and Carol, along with her friend Donna Brown, were excited about the possibility of being hired to work on "The Admiral," a sight-seeing boat that made two cruises per day down the Mississippi river. Because school in Illinois ended earlier than in Missouri, Donna and Carol thought the odds they would get hired were high.

As Donna and Carol were talking about the possibility of landing jobs, Walter's brother, James, appeared at the front screened door of the house, nervously brandishing a pistol in his hand....with alcohol on his breath. He pointed the gun directly at Donna:

"I want to see Walter," he demanded in slurred speech.

Donna was petrified and didn't dare move.

"Dad's not home...don't know where he's at," Carol stammered. James turned, got into an old taxi, and drove away. Carol never found out the reason for this sinister visit.

Through her teens, her father's drinking led to one bizarre episode after another. Working on the Admiral kept her away from the house most of the week, but her father's antics found any opportunity to manifest on her family.

"One day, while Mom was at work, Dad came home and...took Jo Ann and I to a bar in East St. Louis. He drank several beers while Jo Ann and I had sodas. He seemed to be in a good mood," Carol recollects, "We left the bar, but Dad didn't go to his car. Instead he stumbled to the East Saint Louis Jail. We followed him as he walked into the building.

"Lock me up, I want to go to jail!" he insisted to the two policemen sitting at the front. They looked at him and grinned at each other. I didn't understand why he wanted to go to jail!"

"Sure thing, bud! Sounds like a good idea to me," one of the policemen answered.

The other policemen grabbed a set of keys that were hanging on a wall and said,

"Empty your pockets on the counter and follow me."

"Dad emptied his pockets, and as he did so I wondered what the policemen were going to do with Jo Ann and me. I took Jo Ann's hand and gently pulled her toward the front door. Just as we got close to the entrance the other policemen noticed us and shouted,

"Hey, you two, where do you think your going?"

"Run," I whispered to Jo Ann. "We bolted out the wide front door of the police station like two frightened deer and ran as fast as we could up a dark alley that led to where I knew there was a taxi stand. We leaped into the back seat of a taxi and Mom paid the driver when we got home. The next day Dad drove home and acted as if nothing had happened."

Close to her 16th birthday, Carol's grandfather died from emphysema. She was visiting her grandparents the day he went to the hospital, and remembers the day well: "Before Grandpa left, he hesitated and stared at me a long time," she says. "His look gave me a strange premonition feeling."

He would die soon after at the hospital. With her grandmother beside herself with grief, Jo Ann and Carol took turns staying overnight at her house to comfort her.

School started in September, and Carol's mind was on maintaining a high grade-point average. Walter, however, had other things in mind for his family. Carol recalls a terrifying incident that forever changed the way she looked at her father:

"One cold winter night after Dad had been gone a couple of weeks, Jo Ann and I had decided to sleep in Mom's bed with her because our bedroom was so cold. We were awakened by his voice saying, "Anybody moves and I'll slit her throat." I opened my eyes to see Dad standing by the bed, holding a knife at Mom's throat. I was so scared my teeth chattered. I was afraid to move, or do something to provoke Dad to carry out his threat. I've never been so frightened before, or since."

14

On graduation night, June 1957, Carol, was the last student in the class to be called because of her name beginning with a 'W'. As she walked through the gymnasium door, she heard a sobbing sound. Carol looked up at the bleachers and saw her father, drunk and crying.

Carol's hard work in high school finally paid off when she was awarded a full scholarship to any Illinois state university. Being in the top ten per-cent of her class had some benefits, after all!

Despite her generous scholarship, Carol still needed extra money to pay for her boarding and general living expenses while at university. Since she had enjoyed working on the Admiral Excursion Boat the previous summer, Carol decided to return for another summer on the river. Wilma and Jo Ann joined her to bring in extra money.

Another big change in Carol's life was coming this summer: she was finally old enough to learn to drive.

"I had driven Dad's car a few times, starting when I was 14, when he was to inebriated to drive home. Dad's '51 Ford had a stick shift, and I would strip the gears, or just keep the car in the same gear all the way home," she says.

"I studied the driver's handbook like I had never studied a book before. Dad took me on country roads so I could practice driving, and after a few practice drives I felt ready to take the driving test. I passed on my first try."

Walter was lenient with his car but didn't care where his

daughter went, or with whom. Her driving responsibilities began and ended with dropping Walter off at the bar and picking him up before it closed.

That summer Walter had an affair with a woman he met in a bar. His indiscretion bothered Carol more than it bothered her mother. "I think she was glad to have Dad out of her hair," Carol recalls. "Dad had often made fun of Mom's weight, and so it seemed strange to me that his girlfriend, Mildred, was much heavier than Mom."

Carol managed to get Mildred's telephone number and gave the number to all her friends and asked them to call the number often-day or night.

And Carol remembers how she put an end to her fathers philandering: "I was so angry about Dad's unfaithfulness that one night I convinced (some friends) to go with Jo Ann and I to a bar where Dad and his girlfriend hung out. The four of us let the air out of Dad's car tires. Mildred stopped seeing Dad after that."

Carol dated a string of boys that summer, though none were what she would call "serious romances."

"One Friday I went to a party where I met Jim Mundy. I really liked him....thought he was handsome beyond belief. He was tall – six-foot-four – and had a tousled handsomeness with his striking auburn hair, and had teasing, penetrating blue eyes. Also, he had a beautiful ready smile," she recalls.

"After the party Jim invited me to go with him to The Pizza Place. This was the first time I'd tasted pizza and I loved it," she says, "He asked me for another date and I readily accepted. After that we went out again, and again, and I became known as Jim's girl."

"I discovered how much fun he was-he had a lot of nervous energy! Most of the time we went dancing, and he was very good. Since he was so tall, he stood out on the dance floor. Jim got a kick out of the way other couples would leave the dance floor to watch us dance."

Despite a summer of hard work, Carol didn't have enough money to move away for school. She enrolled in the Southern Illinois Branch of Carbondale University in East Saint Louis, and signed up for chemistry, English, and psychology courses.

Carol introduced her friend Mickey Baur to Jim's best friend, Bill Dorman, and they hit it off. The four of them began double-dating at a variety of local jazz clubs.

"We were underage, but this didn't stop us from being served liquor," she says, "I didn't care for the taste of beer, but once I drank the first bottle, the next one didn't taste so bad."

Eventually, her fathers car broke down and this meant Carol no longer had a means of transportation. With a fairly good job working with her mother at the Edison Brothers Shoe Company, she could afford to buy her own car. After a trip to a car dealership, she fell in love with a beautiful red '54 Chevy convertible.

"The dealership sent me to a loan shark where I took out a high interest loan so I could purchase the car," she says. "With car payments, insurance, and $10 per week room and board to Mom, I had very little money left from my paychecks."

Walter eventually decided to move to Alorton, IL, and lived upstairs over a liquor store. He now had very easy access to liquor, running a tab with the store owner. The contractor he worked for picked him up and drove him to construction sites, so he didn't need a car. Not having to pay for a car left him even more money with which to drink.

Carol's romance with Jim also took a turn for the worst around this time. Despite his gift of an elaborate ruby 'promise ring' to her for Christmas, their relationship was nearing its end.

Carol remembers when it all began going downhill:

"While he was at my house he happened to notice all the movie star photos I had taped on the wall of my bedroom. Instead of admiring my collection he remarked, 'How childlike can you get?"

"After he left I yanked the photos from the wall and threw all of them away," she says.

"Soon after, his parents invited Jim and me to go with them to a dinner at their American Legion Post. From the start of the evening it was obvious his mother didn't like me. I was somewhat disinclined to talk with grown-ups, so his Mom and I didn't talk much."

A few days later, Jim broke up with Carol at his mothers urging. Carol was crushed, having lost the man who meant everything to her.

The next day, Carol mailed Jim the beautiful ruby ring he had given her. That evening, several of her friends came by to take her out for the evening in hopes of raising Carol's spirits.

"We're going to Penny's, that new place in Walnut Groves, want to come along?" one of them asked.

"The owner is Don Shaffer," they said. "He drives a Corvette and he's a REAL PRIZE!"

15

"It is said that we don't remember days; we remember moments and I remember the moment I first saw Don Shaffer," Carol says, "I didn't find him exceptionally good looking....he was short, had a receding hairline, walked with a slight limp, and at 28 years old seemed much older than I."

"What he did have, however, was charisma. All the kids at Penney's really liked him, and since he was older they looked up to him as a big brother. He had a great sense of humor, was witty, laughed a lot, and when he did he showed perfect, beautiful white teeth."

When the girls arrived on the scene, the joint was packed. An Elvis Presley song, *You Ain't Nothing But A Hound Dog,* was blaring on a jukebox in a far corner of the huge dance floor.

After Penny's closed at ten o'clock, we went to the Korner Grill, an all night diner located on Route 3. There were quite a few young people there, but Carol was surprised when Don Shaffer rolled up in his Corvette.

"Most of the kids congregated in the parking lot to talk and listen to music on car radios," Carol remembers, "Don strolled over to our car. He flashed his winning smile and asked us our names and where we lived. He was surprised when he found out we actually lived on the same street."

"Before I left Don asked me out for a date that coming

Sunday. I agreed to go and he took me to the Midas Steak House. I had never rode in a corvette, or eaten steak. It was magical....I felt like Cinderella."

"Don and I didn't date during the week," she says, "I was attending college evenings and had homework to do, and had to go to work the next day. We would talk on the telephone, and he'd honk the horn on his car as he drove past my house on his way home after Penny's had closed."

Spring came and the college semester was over. The Cahokia Chamber of Commerce invited Don to drive his car in the homecoming parade on behalf of a junior achievement program. Don was delighted, and asked Carol if she would come with him and throw candy to the kids. "I loved riding in his corvette... liked the way people would look at us when we went by...so I agreed to ride with him in the parade," she remembers.

Carol was having a difficult time making ends meet, so she decided to get her old job on the Admiral Excursion Boat back. Poochie loved to ride in Carol's car, and she took him with her almost everywhere. It wasn't unusual at all then, that she'd take him to fill out a job application.
"It wasn't hot outside, so I was able to leave him in the car while I filled out my application," says Carol.

Carol was on the boat filling out her application when she heard a loud *THUD!* Being on a boat at the time, she didn't think much of it...until a man came dashing into the room looking alarmed. Carol remembers what happened next:
"A car just went into the water!" He shouted.
"A car?" I asked, not really concerned. I continued to fill out the application.
"Yeah, a red convertible...there was a kid in the car!" He said, mistaking a frantic Poochie for a young child.
"Oh my gosh," I stammered, "I have a red convertible!"

Remembering that Poochie was in the car, Carol dashed outside and to the upper deck, looking in vain for her vehicle. It wasn't there!

"Frantic, I ran off the boat and down to the edge of the Mississippi River," Carol says, "There was no sign of my car or dog. I was about to give up hope of ever seeing Poochie again, when suddenly he popped up in the murky water and swam to shore, shaking his fur as he climbed onto land."

Bystanders later told Carol that they had seen a couple of young boys hanging around my car before it went into the river. Someone had called the fire department and a fire truck arrived, though the firemen were glad to hear that they wouldn't have to recover a body from the dangerous river.

Because it was against the law to leave a vehicle in the Mississippi river, Carol's insurance company had to pay a diver to locate the wreck and an extraction team to get it out of the water. Carol was also liable for damage to the Admirals back rudder, damaged in the accident, and had to pay for her car to be towed to a junk yard.

With all the expenses the insurance company had to pay, she barely received enough money to make a down payment on another car. She settled for a '54 Mercury convertible, but would now face an extended period of new car payments. Carol vowed to herself that one day she would win herself a new car, so she wouldn't have to worry about payments. Years later, she would do just that.

Despite the damage to the Admiral, Carol, her mother and Jo Ann were all rehired to work on the boat, but when Summer ended, Carol didn't sign up for any college classes.

"I was bone-tired from holding down two jobs," she

remembers, "I weighed less than 100 pounds, even though I was five-feet-seven-inches tall. I still smoked, and I'm sure this contributed to my being run down."

As the holidays approached, Carol hoped for-almost expected-an engagement ring. It didn't happen. Instead Don gave her a jewelry box. A few months later, he asked her to marry him, and she accepted.

"It seemed like I had been searching for someone like Don all my life...someone I could feel safe with...someone who would take care of me," she says.

"He gave me a much needed feeling of security. Because he was eleven years older than I our relationship was much like a father/daughter relationship. I went along with whatever he wanted to do We got along great with few disagreements."

Carol and Don were married June 18, 1960 at the Cahokia Methodist Church., with Jo Ann serving as Maid of Honor and Mary Simmons, Martha Berry and cousin Linda Van Meter, serving as attendants. Carol, a true romantic, was madly, hopelessly in love, and totally entrusted this man with her happiness, her peace of mind, her life.

Don didn't renew his lease at Penney's. He was ready to settle down and got a job at Emerson Electric Company. He had to start work on the new job the Monday after our wedding, so there would be no honeymoon.

Walter's drinking continued to be a major concern for the Wright family, and on the eve of her marriage, Carol found her father in jail."
The week before the wedding Dad was drinking heavily," says Carol, "Bob Brees (Jo Ann's boyfriend and future husband) was at our house when Dad attempted to strike Jo Ann. Bob came to my sister's defense. Dad hit Bob and his

parents had Dad arrested. Jo Ann and Bob didn't get to attend the rehearsal dinner because they had to meet with a judge and try to arrange for Dad's release from jail. Because of the circumstances, the judge let him get out of jail."

Living with her new husband took some getting used to for Carol, but the newlywed couple made it work. Don took care of the bills and Carol slowly mastered the domestic skills that every housewife at the time was required to know, though she admits that she was "a terrible cook." A short time later, the newly-minted Mr. and Mrs. Shaffer were about to face their first challenge as husband and wife.

"Don's younger brother, 17-year-old Joe, came to live with us two weeks after Don and I were married," says Carol, "Their Dad had kicked him out. Don didn't want Joe to stay with us because he had a reputation as a troublemaker, but I convinced Don to let him move in. This was a big mistake."

When the Shaffer's went away to visit family and friends, Joe held wild parties that resulted in minor property damage. In spite of all this, Don refused to kick his brother out.

"He said I'd wanted him living with us, so now I could figure out a way to get him out," Carol says, "I went to Don's Dad and asked him to allow Joe to move back home because he was causing trouble." This bizarre reasoning managed to persuade Shaffer, and he let his wayward son return home soon after.

Around this time, Wilma left Walter again, this time for good. She took Jo Ann, who had recently graduated from high school, and relocated to Edgemont, Illinois. Eventually, Carol's grandmother would sell her home and pool her resources with Wilma to buy a new home.

Despite numerous incidents of neglect and abuse, Poochie

was still alive, although getting on in years. Unlike the vibrant and playful dog he'd been in his youth, Poochie wasn't eating and just lay around all day. After a trip to the vet, Poochie was diagnosed with throat cancer.

After much soul searching, Wilma and Jo Ann decided it would be best to have Poochie put to sleep to end his suffering. The dog who had survived for years in close proximity to the volatile Walter Wright was finally at peace. He was eighteen and was carefully buried in a metal mail box.

As Poochie's life came to its end, a new life was just beginning. On September 1, 1961, Carol gave birth to her first daughter, Donna.Ruth. Becoming a mother meant the end of her working days for the time being, because Edison Brothers had a company policy that pregnant women could only work up to seven months.

"After Donna was born I didn't return to work. As far as I was concerned, child rearing was as important a job as any other honorable profession and I wanted to do the best at the job of motherhood as I could," Carol explains, "I wanted my baby to grow up in home where love was central, and because of all my turmoil as a child I believed that family was a value that had to be respected and preserved."
Being a mother also provided the opportunity for a new kind of contest:

"One of my favorite TV shows was, *The Charlotte Peters Show*. One day Charlotte announced that she was having "the most beautiful new born baby" contest. I knew all mothers believe their babies are beautiful....and I was no exception! I decided to send Donna's picture to the show and she won! Her picture was shown on the television show and she received a box full of baby gifts."

Like her mother, baby Donna was a natural-born winner.

16

Despite giving up her opportunity for a free college education and leaving the workplace, Carol was content in married life. When Donna turned three, Carol gave birth to another beautiful daughter. Diana Lynn Shaffer was born on February 24th, 1964. "Donna adored her little sister," says Carol, "It was my hope that they would grow up to be as close as Jo Ann and I had always been."

Jo Ann was due to be married herself to her longtime paramour, Bob Brees. Unfortunately, trouble marred this wedding as well, as Carol recalls: "Dad refused to give Jo Ann away because she wouldn't invite his brother, James, to the wedding," she says, "Bob's Dad walked Jo Ann down the aisle, even though he had recently broken his leg and it was in a cast."

By now, Don had become a civil servant in the employ of the federal government, working for the US Army as an industrial engineer. Because his job required extensive travel around the country, Carol found herself shouldering much of the responsibilities at home. Carol considered "motherhood" to be her career.

"My goal was to be the best parent possible," she says, "I didn't have much time to enter contests, but one day I saw an essay contest mentioned in the local newspaper that piqued my interest." Illinois State Senator Ralph Dunn challenged his constituents to write him a speech, and Carol decided to take him up on it. Carol won the contest and received a small monetary prize and a silver collector's coin with Senator Dunn's picture on it.

Three months after Diana was born. Don came home from work with a bombshell to drop on his wife: Don's superiors had appointed him to staff a position in Toronto, Ontario, Canada, hundreds of miles away! Carol was stunned.

"Toronto? Why Toronto?" she asked, "It's so far away."
Don explained that in order for him to advance in his career he had to be flexible and willing to relocate.

"I didn't want to move so far away from Cahokia," Carol says. "My mother and Jo Ann doted on Donna and Diana. The timing was not propitious. I felt like my world was spinning the wrong way."

Don, however, was firm. "I can't do it. I can't move so far away," Carol pleaded.
"Yes you can," he said, his tone allowing no argument.
"Besides, we'll only be gone one year," said Don, "We won't sell the house, but rent it while we're gone. I'll ask Bob and Jo Ann to manage the property."

The Shaffers moved to Toronto and Carol was launched into a whole new world, riding streetcars during the day while Don was at work. Don received a generous housing allowance and he was encouraged to use it. Upon moving to Toronto, the couple took up residence in a hotel and looked for a house to rent. Before long, Don's superior at work, Colonel Demory, invited Carol and her husband to stay with him. After a stay with the Colonel and his military family, the Shaffers soon immigrated to the Toronto neighborhood of Etobicoke and rented a beautiful upscale home.

The year went by but Don didn't receive orders to return to St. Louis. Instead he had to attend a school at Fort Eustis, Virginia. Carol and the girls went with him for the two weeks. They ended up living in Toronto for three years and during that time Don often had to go to government schools.

After a while, Don was assigned to the state department in Ottawa. "There was a housing shortage in the capital," Carol recalls, "So we rented a trailer in Stittsville, Ontario, while we looked for a house to rent."

Carol and her family liked living in the trailer park so much that they decided to purchase their own mobile home. Don's housing allowance rules weren't as stringent in Ottawa, so he was able to use the allowance to purchase a trailer and pay rental fee for a space in the park. Carol recalls this time fondly and remembers happily participating in a Women's Club that spearheaded community improvement projects and fundraisers. The family also got a dog, Bobo, a poodle.

Carol was beginning to enjoy the challenges of living far from home. There was a junior college located on the outskirts of Ottawa, where she enrolled in a several non-credit evening classes – gourmet cooking, interior decorating, and a self-improvement course where Carol learned how to dress in a cosmopolitan, stylish manner. The information Carol gained from these courses gave her the confidence to host parties for Don's fellow American co-workers, and their spouses, and for their Canadian friends.

"Our first party was a dinner party for Don's co-workers and spouses," Carol remembers, "I prepared several recipes I had learned in my gourmet cooking class. They loved my dishes and some asked for the recipes. After dinner we played charades and everyone had such a good time it was well after midnight before they went home."

"At Christmas I reserved the recreational center and decorated it with decorations that I convinced a local grocery store owner to donate for a Christmas party," Carol says, "We invited our American and Canadian friends and all seemed to enjoy the camaraderie."

"One day I saw an ad in the Ottawa Newspaper stating that a local theater group was forming and they were looking for members," she says, "The director was a high school drama teacher and several radio personalities were already members."

Carol joined the theater group for its production of *Barefoot in the Park,* but was relegated to the props department because of her strong southern accent. In spite of this, she was promised a speaking role if they produced, *A Cat On A Hot Tin Roof.* This experience gave Carol a lifelong love of the theater. Her contesting endeavors would eventually take her to performances of *Mama Mia, Hairspray, Jesus Christ Superstar, Phantom of the Opera* and *Little Women.*

Since Don had a job with the state department, Carol got to attend various state functions. "One of the first functions we attended was a birthday celebration for the United States Marine Corps held at the U.S. Embassy," she says, "The Embassy was decorated in blue and gold velvets and red silks – and the food was delicious!"

Despite this, Carol was surprised when one day a courier hand delivered two invitations from the Governor General of Canada to attend a garden party at the Governor's mansion. The seal of the English Crown was on the invitation.

"Don wasn't able to attend because of a project he was working on," says Carol, "So I invited (my Canadian friend) Marion Melnechuk to attend with me. She was thrilled. When we arrived I saw several white tents that dotted the grounds of the mansion. Marion and I waited in a line with some dignitaries to meet the Governor General. After the introduction, Marion and I found a seat at one of the tables and indulged in a delicious lunch."

Carol and Don had been living in Ottawa for two years when there was a change of command. The new commander in charge of Don's office was Colonel William Cornwell.

"The Cornwells hosted a party at their house for everyone in the office and their spouses," Carol recalls, "It was a very elegant party. When we arrived we were met by a liveried servant who opened the door for us. Food was catered and several magnums of champagne were served. This was a far cry from the life I'd lived at Maplewood Park!"

Despite living in Canada far longer than she intended to, Carol's family journeyed north several times to visit friends. On one of the trips north, Jo Ann, Bob, Wilma and Carol's grandmother got more than they bargained for:

"A week before they arrived someone had shot a hole in the side of our mobile home," says Carol, "The local police believed it was probably an anti-American act protesting the war in Vietnam. It was a time of unrest – with draft dodgers and some Canadians protesting the war along with civil rights infractions involving Black people in the United States."

A few months after their return home, Carol received a letter from Jo Ann announcing that she was pregnant. Not all the news was happy ... Jo Ann wrote that Walter had shown up at their house so ill he could hardly walk. She hand fed him and nursed him back to good health, and he was now staying with his daughter and her husband.

"On April 25, 1968 I received a telephone call from Bob to tell me the exciting news that Jo Ann had given birth to a baby boy they named Robert Lloyd Brees, Junior," says Carol.

Don's duties took him far from home, and he frequently flew out of the Ottawa airport on business trips. Carol remembers one experience as she saw her husband off: "Once while I was waiting I looked up to see, sitting across from me, Canada's Prime Minister, Pierre Trudeau. Our eyes locked for a long time and when he got up to leave he smiled. I thought he had an interesting face."

17

Tragedy has no time table and can strike anytime, anywhere. On a cold Sunday morning Don's sister called to inform the Shaffer's that Don's father had been killed in a train crash back home in Illinois. A train engineer, his engine had collided head-on with another.

"The night of the crash I was awakened by a spooky chill in our bedroom," remembers Carol, "Don didn't wake up, but he did stir in his sleep. I glanced at an alarm clock on a table next to the bed to see what time it was and then went back to sleep." She later calculated that with the time difference, this was the exact time when her father-in-law was killed.

"I'm inclined to believe that the chill I felt in the bedroom was his father's spirit," she says, "We immediately flew home for the funeral and stayed for a week."

Shortly after the Shaffer's returned to Canada, Don received orders that he was being transferred to Stuart, Florida. Though disappointed that she was not being sent back to St. Louis, Carol was excited about the prospect of moving to Florida: at almost 31 years old, she had never even seen the ocean. Carol and Don had made Canada their home for seven years. Before leaving, Don took advantage of his job's special standing to buy a Chrysler duty free and tax free from Detroit.

On the way to Florida, the Shaffer family stopped in Indiana and bought a camper-trailer. They then went to Cahokia to visit relatives and see Carol's newborn nephew. Walter still lived with Jo Ann and was thrilled to have a grandson. After three days in Illinois, it was off to Florida.

"Somewhere along Florida's coastline I saw the Atlantic Ocean," Carol says, "It was awesome! I couldn't get over the vastness of it, or the loudness of the waves. We ran barefoot along the beach – Bobo was as excited as the rest of us." The Shaffers rented a space in a small trailer park on the outskirts of Stuart, Florida, and made themselves at home.

After Don got settled in at work, he and Carol went house-hunting. They soon found a new subdivision, under construction, and quickly bought a property.

"We chose a three bedroom ranch style home," says Carol, "We picked a corner lot with a lemon tree and an orange tree in the back...to build the house on. While our house was under construction we would live in the trailer." After what seemed like forever, construction on the new house was complete, and the Shaffer's moved in ... parting forever with their mobile home. "It is one thing to go camping in a trailer but another to actually live in one for several months."

When school started Donna tested so high she skipped the third grade and was put in the fourth grade. Diana would be starting first grade and both girls were excited about going to school. The week before Halloween, the girls brought home notes that there would be a Halloween costume contest at school...an event right up Carol's alley.

"I did my best to come up with a design for two winning costumes," she recalls, "The first thing I did was look around the house for interesting props that I could use because I know props will enhance the look of a costume. My mother had sent Donna a musical zither for her birthday and I decided to make Donna a Greek Goddess costume to go with her zither. I sewed her Goddess dress from an old white sheet, and made Donna's long hair appear even longer by attaching my own "fall" hairpiece to her locks. I braided the hair with gold drapery rope and used a piece of the rope as a belt for the dress. I completed the Goddess outfit by spraying a pair of Donna's old sandals with gold paint."

"I created an 'outer space' costume for Diana. I sewed her space suit from cheap silver cloth and made her a helmet from my aluminum kitchen colander. I painted a 3rd eye on her forehead and for the eye's eyelashes I glued on a false eyelash over the fake eye. I completed her costume by covering her rain boots with aluminum foil."

Both girls won first places in their grades and received prizes. For Carol, the experience took her back to the costume contests of her youth. Around the same time, Carol learned that she was pregnant again.

Six months into her pregnancy, Don learned he was being transferred in about three months... to either Phoenix, Arizona or back home to St. Louis.

While she was overjoyed that there was a prospect of soon returning home, Carol was still concerned. "In three months I would be nine months pregnant, she says, "And I didn't know if my baby would be born in Phoenix or St. Louis. I liked my obstetrician in Stuart and hoped my child would be born in Florida."

Carol got her wish. Don's transfer was delayed and on May 20, 1971 their newborn son, Donald Leslie Shaffer II, came into the world. Since she had never had a brother, Carol always hoped to have a boy someday. At 31 years old, she felt that her family was complete.

A few months later Don came home bursting with excitement. Embracing his wife in a tight hug, he gave her the good news: "I'm being transferred back to St. Louis, not Phoenix," he said. Carol couldn't believe it ... she was finally going home. For a while the family lived at their old house at Maplewood Park. The two-bedroom house was too small and the neighborhood had changed into a rundown community.

To be close to Don's family, the Shaffers moved to Columbia, Illinois, and bought a new split-level home. Carol's mother and grandmother eventually relocated to Columbia as well, after Wilma was beaten and mugged after stepping off a bus in Edgemont.

"At first it was difficult to make friends in Columbia because it is such a tight knit community. Outsiders weren't particularly welcomed," says Carol, "One day I saw an ad in the local newspaper that the Columbia Woman's Club was seeking new members. I convinced Don's sister, Dana, to attend a meeting with me. The women in the club weren't very cordial to us and Dana refused to go back."

Carol refused to give up so easily, and went back the next month. This time the members were more receptive and she joined the club, becoming chairwoman of the decorating committee for a graduating student's brunch.

The event was a huge success and through the years Carol went on to serve on various committees, and eventually became an officer of the club. She found Columbia Woman's Club to be a superb social organization for women, very much like the Woman's Club she'd belonged to in Stittsville, Ontario… but on a much bigger scale.

18

With her daughters at school and a newborn at home, Carol had her hands full for the first several months in Columbia. Despite this, she always found time to do what she loved best: contesting.

"When I heard an announcement on KMOX Radio that the station was sponsoring a sweepstakes for their charity Christmas show, I knew I would enter," Carol says, "The prize was a speaking part in the show for the winner and a friend. KMOX is my favourite radio station so I thought it would be great to get to meet all the radio personalities and be able to put a face to the announcers that I listened to almost every day."

The rules for the sweepstakes required contestants to mail a postcard to the radio station with the contestant's name, address, and telephone number printed on the postcard. To make her postcard stand out from the rest, Carol decorated her postcard with a Santa Claus singing into a microphone, as if he was singing on the radio.

"My postcard must have caught the attention of the judges," Carol recounts, "because I was called by telephone and told I had won. I was also informed that there would be a rehearsal the night before the live performance. My friend Carol Giffhorn agreed to participate in the show with me.

"My part called for me to scream because radio personality, Jim White, had stolen my cheese sandwich. I was worried that radio listeners wouldn't be able to hear me, so I screamed as loud as I possibly could into a very sensitive radio microphone. When I screamed the radio engineer fell off a stool he was sitting on and exclaimed, "You blew the earwax right out of my ears!"

"Embarrassed, I asked if I should tone my scream for the live broadcast. "Oh no", he said. "It was great, and I'll be better prepared for it the next time."

The day of the show KMOX ran promotions all day with an announcer saying, "Tune in tonight folks for our Holiday Christmas Show and hear Carol Shaffer scream!" The show was a huge success, and that Christmas season, Carol's legendary scream filled the airwaves of the Midwest.

Like most radio shows, KMOX sponsored new contests every week to engage its listeners. Carol recounts how she won her first cooking contest after KMOX asked listeners to mail in their favourite barbeque recipes to the station: "My strategy was to use unusual ingredients in my sauce....soy sauce and mango juice...and my recipe was one of the ten chosen." She won, and got to compete in a cook-off at the radio station the following week. "I had never grilled before so Donna's husband Bob gave me a quick lesson on barbequing."

"As the contestants grilled their meat, an enthusiastic announcer interviewed us," says Carol, "He asked me, "Why do you think your sauce is so good?"
"My bar-b-que sauce is so good it will marinate a brick."
I told him, hoping my humour would help to get me chosen as the winner. It must have worked, because I won. My prize was a big meat smoker."

Like many women around the world, young and old, Carol had always wanted to go to Paris, France. When she saw the "Lorraine Cheese Sandwich Contest" entry blanks at a supermarket deli counter with the grand prize of a trip to Paris, she decided to enter the contest. Her strategy was to submit several sandwich combinations...always making sure to include Lorraine Cheese in the sandwiches. She didn't win the grand prize trip to Paris, but won First Prize – a bread-maker – and also cemented a basic strategy to win any cooking contest:

1. Prepare the recipe carefully, and make sure to give the exact measurements for the ingredients and the correct cooking time.
2. Use the sponsor's product/products in the recipe.
3. Don't choose a recipe that has too many ingredients. (People are busy and prefer fast, easy to prepare recipes).
4. Use ingredients that are available in most grocery stores. (People don't have time to go looking for unusual ingredients).
5. Give the recipe a catchy name.
6. Test the recipe on family or friends before submitting it.
7. Keep abreast of food fads by reading current magazines and cookbooks.
8. Be creative. Experiment with unusual food combinations. This is one of the best ways to pick up those extra points so helpful in winning cooking contests.
9. Check recipe thoroughly to make sure there aren't any mistakes before mailing it.

As for Paris, the *City of Light* could wait...Carol would make it there eventually.

By this time, Walter no longer lived with Jo Ann and Bob. He moved to Okawville, Illinois to manage a small farm owned by Jo Ann's in-laws. Walter loved the farm and lived there for four years, finding peace by taking care of the animals and enjoying the outdoors. In an ironic twist of fate, he became fond of an oversized farm dog named "King", and was heartbroken when he found the dog shot...a far cry from the night he'd callously tried to kill his family's dog, Poochie.

"Jo Ann and I liked to take the kids to Okawville so they could experience life on the farm," says Carol. "Once I brought a camera with me and took a photo of Dad and Donald feeding and petting baby pigs. I entered the photograph in the Monroe County Fair and it won first place. I believe it is possible to enhance the odds of winning a photograph contest if there are children or animals in the photo."

When the time came to sell the farm, Walter needed a place to live. Bob and Jo Ann had housed him while Carol was away, so Carol invited him to stay with her family. Walter caused very few problems ("He knew better," says Carol), and was respectful of Carol and Don's home.

"Jo Ann and I couldn't put Dad out on the street," explains Carol, "He would most certainly have been a homeless person. Every once in awhile he would find an odd job and get enough money to buy a few beers. Don would be openly critical and make remarks to our friends such as, "Well, looks like he's got a snoot full tonight."

Don decided to buy a small trailer park in Sauget, Illinois, as an investment, and Walter offered to live at the park as the handyman. Don bought him a used mobile home.

But before Walter could move into the trailer he fell ill. At the hospital, he was diagnosed with pneumonia. Despite a brave fight, he died two days after hospitalization Carol and Jo Ann at his side.. He was buried as a veteran with full military honours.

Despite her difficult years with her father, Carol was deeply moved by his death.
"It was the end of an era," Carol notes. "When my nephew Bobby was 14 years old, Joann and Bob adopted William Anthony 'Tony' Brees."

19

Involvement in the community was important to Carol. She wanted her family to belong to a local swimming association so that her children could learn to swim, but Don wasn't in agreement, deeming it too costly. This proved to be a catalyst for Carol to rejoin the workforce. She got a job as a sales clerk at the Famous Barr Department Store in St. Louis to help pay for the membership. When Donna and Diana needed braces, Carol's newfound income helped pay for down-payments.

Unlike her mother, Donna didn't grow up in a family struggling to make ends meet. Like her mother, however, Donna found contesting an ideal way to add adventure to life. Following in Carol's footsteps, Donna entered and won an essay contest when she was a sophomore in high school. "She wrote her essay in an interesting style, utilizing all the facts she had found, and of course, came up with a catchy opening sentence," says Carol.

Donna's prize was a trip to Washington D.C. Two Sophomore students from each state won and the group toured the nation's capital, and shook hands with President Carter. Carol passed on her essay-writing knowledge to her daughter, who found it as easy to follow and as useful as she did. Having entered many essay contests over the years, Carol has noticed a common trend that makes winning easier than some would think:

"Few people enter essay contests because they feel it is too much work, or they fear they aren't smart enough to win," she says. "Since I like to write, I'm glad that people are intimidated by essay contests because it means I'll have a greater chance of winning."

"The reason there aren't as many essay contests is because sweepstakes generally create more interest and are much simpler for a sponsor to conduct," Carol explains. "An essay contest requires the sponsor to do more work because the entries have to be individually read and judged."

When the opportunity came to enter an essay contest sponsored by her favorite soap opera, *The Young and the Restless,* Carol leapt into action. The prize was a guest appearance on a commercial to promote the program. The rules were simple: Write a hundred words or less on their favorite character on the show.

"I assumed that the contestants would be writing about the (protagonists), the stars of the show," says Carol. "My strategy was to be different, to stand out and be noticed. I wrote about Jill Abbott, the trouble maker on the show. It wasn't easy to come up with endearing qualities about Jill Abbott, but I must have because I won the contest."

Carol also used essay writing contests as opportunities to point out benevolent acts that often would otherwise go unrecognized: "Circuit City was sponsoring an essay contest to honor local heroes," she says. "I wrote an essay about my daughter, Diana, describing how her quick thinking and actions saved a young man's life. She was driving to work and came upon an accident scene where a motorcyclist was struck by a car. Without any regard for her own safety, Diana angled her car to protect the injured motorcyclist from being hit by on-coming traffic. Diana is a nurse, and she knew how to administer first aid and she stayed with the injured man until an ambulance arrived. The essay won and Diana received a $100 gift card from Circuit City."

"One of the things I like about "contesting" as a hobby is that it enables me to do special things for my family," says Carol, "In May 2004 Diana was named a "ChAnnl Woman of Influence." I nominated her in an essay contest I'd heard about...the rules for the contest called for an essay explaining why their nominee deserved the honor of being a "ChAnnl Woman of Influence."

Carol felt Diana had an excellent chance of being chosen for humanitarian reasons. She had just returned from a missionary trip to Mexico where she and her family had helped to build a home for a Mexican family that was living in a car.

"In the essay I also mentioned how Diana had been named the employee of the month at the hospital where she works and was nominated to be Missouri Nurse of the Year. I printed the essay on computer paper that had a pretty flowery border, hoping to enhance the odds of winning. After all, this was for ChAnnl."

It worked! Carol's essay won and Diana was invited to an awards dinner at the elegant Coronado Hotel in St. Louis. Diana was given several ChAnnl products and other nice gifts at the presentation.

On June 17, 2004, Donald became part of history as he carried the Olympic Torch for a leg of its journey in St. Louis on its way to Athens, Greece. St. Louis was one of four cities in the country to have the torch. Donald was chosen to be a torch bearer in a national essay contest sponsored by Coca-Cola. He was nominated by his sister, Donna.

The contest asked the contestants to describe why their candidate was inspirational by taking joy in life and portraying a positive attitude which lifts the spirits of those around them; being the extraordinary ordinary person who proves that one individual can make a difference; embracing history and culture and passing the lessons learned from one generation to the next; and actively seeking to experience life's adventures and challenges big and small.

Donald is a professional firefighter for Central County Fire Department in St. Peters, Missouri, so Donna's strategy was to write how the Olympic flame was symbolic for her brother's career. She wrote how he's used to putting out flames...not running with them... how instead of putting the fire out he would make sure to keep the Olympic flame lit.

When a reporter asked him if he wanted to sprint or just take a light jog with the flame, Donald said, "I think I will take it slow and savor the opportunity because it will probably never happen again

As Donald learned he would be carrying the Olympic Torch in St. Louis, Carol was excited that she'd won a trip for two to the 2004 Summer Olympics in Athens as part of another sweepstakes sponsored by Coca-Cola.

"My strategy for this sweepstakes was to mail an entry everyday for a month... the rules stated I could enter as often as I wished as long as each entry was in a separate envelope," Carol says.

Carol was seated in front of the vault where American gymnast Paul Hamm won the gold medal. She took time to visit the sights of Athens, the Acropolis and the Parthenon among them.

"With a hobby like this, I never know what the future holds," says Carol, "Not in my wildest dreams did I ever imagine that my son would someday carry the Olympic Torch or that I would travel to Athens, Greece and attend the Olympic Games. With contesting, anything is possible!"

20

Despite her string of wins in local sweepstakes and contests, Carol and her like-minded brood knew where the real money lay in wait...Hollywood.

"One day Jo Ann, Donna, Mom, and I got the bright idea that we'd like to go to Los Angeles and try out for game shows," says Carol, "The problem with our idea was that we didn't know how we could finance the trip since none of us worked at the time."

After a brainstorming session, the resourceful quartet decided to raise funds by making and selling crafts, and baking and decorating cookies, which they sold to a nursing home.

"It took two years before we had saved enough money to make the trip to Los Angeles," says Carol, "We purposely scheduled our trip according to the audition days at the game shows. Mom, Jo Ann, Tony (Jo Ann's son), Donna, Amanda (Donna's daughter), and I made the journey, and while we were there we treated ourselves to a Hollywood/Beverly Hills tour, a day at Disneyland and Universal Studios, and a visit to Sea World at San Diego."

The first game show the troupe auditioned for was *Wheel of Fortune*. Jo Ann and Wilma weren't enthusiastic, but Carol and her daughter were willing to give it a shot.

At the audition there was a long line of hopefuls, from which groups of about twenty people would be called into a room that had rows of desk, where they were given a written test to complete.

Winning Big

"The test consisted of three pages of puzzles," says Carol, "We were told to solve as many puzzles as possible in only five minutes. If we only knew a part of a puzzle...perhaps only the first or last name of a person or the name of a city, but not the state...we were told to write in the portion we knew and then go on to the next puzzle."

Those who solved at least eight puzzles were eligible to advance to the next step in the screening process. While Carol didn't make the cut, her daughter, Donna, did.

Donna and the nine semi-finalists were taken to a room where there was a mock *Wheel of Fortune* wheel. They had to play a pretend game using pretend money and pretend prizes. Carol believes the purpose of this round was to gauge the reactions of contestants as they would appear on the show, no matter who won or lost.

"Before we had left home Donna had read an article stating how the producers of game shows look for contestants with outgoing personalities," says Carol, "She did her best to appear enthusiastic."

After the mock game, there was a brief interview with a producer asking the semi-finalist to tell them a little about themselves.

While some gave bland, formulaic responses, Donna heeded her mothers' advice to stand out and be noticed: When it was her turn to speak, she jumped up like a cheerleader and exclaimed, "I baked 10,000 cookies to get here!"

"Her answer got the producer's attention and they asked her to explain," Says Carol, "All bubbly and perky, she told how she, her mom, aunt, and grand-ma had financed their trip to California by baking and selling cookies. She explained how friends had said we'd never make it, but their doubt had made us even more determined. Donna is convinced that it was her story that won her a spot on the show."

The ten semi-finalists became three finalists, but Donna and the others didn't know it until long after their return to Illinois.

Thinking they had returned home empty-handed, Carol and her family were overjoyed to receive a letter informing Donna of her status and giving her a date to appear on the show. Carol recounts the vigorous process of preparing a game show taping:

"The day of the taping she had to be at the studio at 7 AM, even though the show wouldn't be taped until 5 PM." says Carol, "The producers were very precise about what they wanted her to do. She was told where to look, where not to look. They told her...you better not do this, you better not do that. Donna found it difficult to be enthusiastic and spontaneous with so much to remember. If she had family members in the audience she wasn't permitted to speak, or look at them during the taping. If she did she would be disqualified."

With years of hard work on the line, Donna prepared to make her television debut...and didn't dare disobey the producer's instructions.

21

When the lights, camera, and action kicked into gear, Donna was on the spot, but fared well against her competition. Through the rounds of the show, she solved the puzzles and emerged as the grand prize winner of the game.

Donna won carpeting, pots and pans, a kitchen range, and a wine rack. As the big winner, she had the opportunity to try and solve a puzzle at the end of the show to win the grand prize...a trip for two to Paris, France. Donna solved the puzzle and won the trip.

Donna was extremely lucky for the opportunity to be on the game show: every year, over a million people try out for *Wheel of Fortune*, but only about 600 make it to the final round.

The odds are stacked against making it to the end; with even the producers of the show strongly discourage anyone from spending a lot of money to travel to California to try out, but Donna proved it can be done. Beating the odds to make it to Hollywood, she soon came under the spotlight of the local media as well. Reporters from local newspapers and radio stations interviewed her during her moment in the sun.

While Donna was fighting hard to make it onto *Wheel of Fortune,* Carol and Jo Ann decided to try their luck elsewhere, making their way to CBS Television studios in hopes of appearing on *The Price is Right.*

"We had to be at the studio before 7:30 in the morning where seating is on a first come, first seated basis," says Carol,

"A producer asked us a few questions and then had us walk a short distance. I am guessing they wanted to see how we'd look if we "came on down!"

Jo Ann and Carol returned on time for the taping, but weren't called down from the audience to appear as contestants. "I hadn't followed my own advice to stand out and be noticed," She says, "We were dressed conservatively, but the people who were picked were dressed to stand out from the crowd. I'd goofed!"

Fortunately, Carol did get to be a contestant on the game show *To Tell the Truth* after an article about her contesting endeavors appeared in *Good Housekeeping* magazine, with the producers actively seeking her out for an appearance. The producer explained that the show, which had been popular years ago, was being brought back with a twist: To win the big prize contestants have to fool the studio audience, as well as a celebrity panel.

To Tell the Truth is taped at the NBC Studios in Burbank, California. After arriving in Burbank, Carol was taken to a studio where she met the two women who would be impersonating her as "Carol Shaffer, The Contest Queen."

Both women, one a UCLA professor and the other a paralegal, were well prepared for their roles. Carol mailed them a copy of her *Win Big* video to study. was coached in ways to fool the audience, told to talk less and make herself less conspicuous on air...not an easy task. Though she was unsure of her performance during the taping, Carol pull it off, stumping the celebrity panel and studio audience...winning $10,000!

"Being a contestant on a game show is a lot of fun! It isn't an impossible goal," says Carol, "All it takes is the will to find a way to make it happen, and you can have a once in a lifetime experience!

Carol's parents, Walter and Wilma Wright

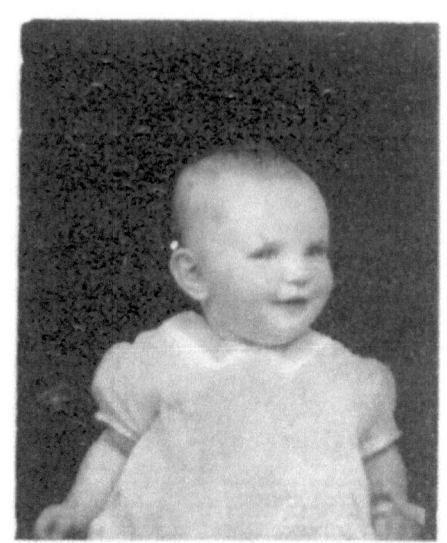

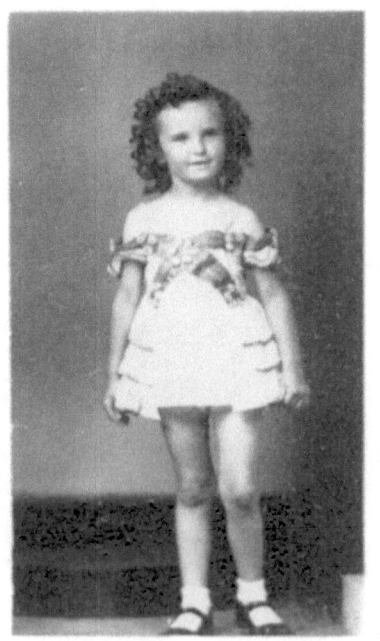

Carol as a giggling baby and as a youthful tap dancer

Carol's student ID card... and her childhood home on Mildred Avenue at Maplewood Park where she spent her teens

Carol as a young woman with a fetching smile

Winning Big

Carol with the LHS Chrysler she won… and with To Tell The Truth game show MC John O-Hurley (from Seinfeld). Carol was the show's big winner – she spent her winnings on a trip to China.

Winning Big

Carol with Ed Reinbold on the Great Wall of China… and at a Chinese Wal-Mart

Winning Big

Carol gets playful with a kangaroo after winning a trip to the 2002 Olympics in Australia ... Carol and Ed Reinbold relax at the Parthenon at Athens, after winning a trip to the 2004 Olympics in Greece.

Carol and her daughter Diana Richardson flank Oprah Winfrey after Carol won a trip to Chicago to meet the legendary talk show host, attend two show tapings and dine with Oprah... Carol admires vintage car on the set of King of the Hill after she won a role as an extra in the Hollywood movie.

22

"Life is not a dress rehearsal," says Carol, "When I turned forty (in 1979), I saw the birthday as a milestone, a time to take stock of what I wanted to do with the rest of my life. I feared I'd wake up one day in my 70's or 80's and regret all the things I'd never done."

Carol made a list of "dreams" that she wanted to make come true. When she, finished Carol had twenty "dreams" on her list and was determined to make every single one come true. "I believed that I had chosen a direction for my future and now I needed to start building on it," she says, "I wished I had started sooner...but luckily, I have never been afraid of failure."

The first item on her list was the most obvious: "GO BACK TO COLLEGE."

"If I wanted to enroll in college I'd have to pay for the tuition and books myself," says Carol, " So I got a job doing demo work at a local grocery store. I used the money I earned to pursue a marketing degree. I could only afford two or three classes per semester, but I did attend classes all year. It felt wonderful to be back in a classroom."

That summer added another win to her string of sweepstakes victories, this time the prize was a Mississippi River cruise for two on the Becky Thatcher Riverboat with local radio personality, Jim White.

"The rules for the sweepstakes called for listeners to mail a postcard to the radio station with their name, address, and telephone number printed on their postcard," says Carol, "I went a step further and drew a picture of a boat on my postcard and printed "Patty Wagon" on the side of the boat that I'd drawn. On air, Jim often talked about his boat and said he had named it for his wife, Patty."

While enjoying her cruise on the *Thatcher,* Carol was surprised to see Captain Bill Carroll on board. Captain Carroll had been her boss when a teenage Carol had worked on the SS Admiral Excursion boat. Captain Carroll remembered his former employee and the two chatted about the old days, particularly how Carol's car had rolled into the Mississippi River and hit a rudder of the boat. "I'm sure he didn't chuckled the day it happened although he didn't fire me," she says

On June 6, 1990, Carol graduated college... with honors.

"I agree with Jennifer Lopez who said, 'Life is about two things....loving and learning.' I considered the years I spent at college well spent, and except when I had my children, among the happiest days of my life," Carol says.

To ensure a high final mark in her marketing program, Carol elected to make "Contests, Sweepstakes and Promotions" the subject of her graduating thesis. "I had been entering contests, sweepstakes, and occasionally a promotion for most of my life, but I found I had much to learn on the subject," says Carol.

A lifetime of entering contests has given Carol intimate insight into promotions and their use in marketing...as well as some of the pitfalls waiting for the unwary participant. She points to timeshare promotions as a potential payoff, but also as a potentially serious problem for a would-be investor.

"Contests are one thing," she says. "A promotion, however, is a horse of a different color because you have to give some sort of consideration. It might be money, or perhaps your time listening to a sales presentation. In return participants are given something ...I was able to visit Las Vegas and Orlando after I attended two separate timeshare promotions, including a tour of the developments. I didn't purchase a time share, but I was given airline tickets for participating in the promotion."

Some of Carol's family gave in to the lure of timeshare promoters: "Jo Ann and her husband decided they would attend a promotion as well and succumbed to the fast talking, high pressure sales people they encountered and purchased a time share. The fine print of their contract stated they had 24 hours to change their minds. They reconsidered and cancelled the contract."

Despite this, two of Carol's children, Diana and Donald, currently own timeshares and consider them to be good investments for their families.

Carol asserts it's important for people to know the difference between promotions and sweepstakes, to keep from being disappointed.

"Promotions are not a fraudulent sales technique as long as the terms of the offer are clear," she says. "Unfortunately, promotions are often confused with sweepstakes, especially if the promotion is in the form of a congratulatory letter stating, "Congratulations! You've won a fabulous trip to Florida." When a recipient of the letter calls a telephone number that is given in the letter, he or she is told that a "processing fee" is required in order to receive the trip. The "processing fee" is often more than the value of the trip."

"Another promotion strategy is when a person receives a congratulatory letter asking the recipient of the letter to call a 900 telephone number to claim a prize. (900 numbers are not toll-free). Generally speaking, if I have to spend any money, buy a product, post a deposit, pay any fees to claim a prize, beyond taxes, I don't participate."

Although Carol has won many contests and sweepstakes through the years, she was unfamiliar with what actually goes on behind the scenes. "I learned that judging a contest can be dull and repetitive, that judges are like anyone else...

attracted to anything unusual or colorful," she says, "If they see an entry blank that is interesting or colorful they are drawn to it. As I had already known, color is powerful. A color newspaper ad can be up to 80% more effective than a black and white ad...especially if the colors are red, orange, or yellow."

"It is a known fact that color gets attention," says Carol, "Marketing departments of major companies have spent millions of dollars to research which colors to put on their packaging to influence people to buy that product."

Carol also learned that judges look for neatness, and are turned off by ink smears or soiled entries. Judges don't want to have to struggle to read an entry, and instead they will simply choose a different entry blank.

"I was surprised to learn that as many as 25% of all contests and sweepstakes entries are disqualified because the people who enter them are too busy, or too lazy, to take the time to read the rules," Carol explains.

"Rules help judges to judge a contest or pick a sweepstakes and to be fair about it," says Carol, "By reading and following the rules; you gain a huge edge over all the competition."

These are examples of what to look for in the official rules of a contest or sweepstakes:

1) Rules should state when a contest or sweepstakes begins and ends, and if the entry must be received by a postmark date or by a deadline date. A short deadline date offers a better chance of success because there will probably be fewer entries. During the summer vacation months, and at Christmas when people are busy, there aren't as many entries either.

2) Rules should state when and how a winner or winners will be chosen, and once a winner or winners are chosen how they

will be notified.

3) Rules should list the terms, conditions, and eligibility requirements for a contest or sweepstakes. The list should include a complete description of the prizes and estimated retail value of non-cash prizes. The rules should make it clear that if there is a cash option available instead of accepting a merchandise prize. If the prize is cash, the rules should state if the money will be offered in a single cash payment or in installments. If there is a grand prize the rules should state if it goes to only one winner, or is it possible the prize will have to be shared by more than one winner.

4) Rules should state if a purchase is necessary in order to enter and this information should be on both the entry form and in the official rules. Since the element of chance has been eliminated in a contest, it is acceptable for a sponsor in some states to request a contestant to buy something or require an entry fee, though they seldom do. Some of these states are Arizona, Arkansas, California, Connecticut, Florida, Iowa, Minnesota, Maryland, New Mexico, and Vermont. In Iowa an entry form has to state, "You must pay $ to compete for this prize." The laws change from state to state, so it's a good idea to learn the laws where you live. In the event a proof of purchase is required, do not staple or tape the proof of purchase to the entry blank because this could cause the entry to be disqualified.

5) Rules should include the estimated odds of winning the prize....odds are often based on the number of entries received. If the odds of winning a prize are listed at 1:1, this means that everyone who enters will win a prize.

6) Rules should include the name and address of the sponsor of the contest or sweepstakes and/or the address where contestants can write to request a list of winners.

7) Rules should state the sponsor's publicity rights regarding

the use of the winner or winner's names.

8) Rules should state if another form of entry, such as a postcard, is allowed. If there aren't anymore entry blanks available at the sponsor's display site, there are usually rules on the display board stating if a 3"x 5" index card can be used as an entry blank. Sometimes there will be an address where people can write to request an entry form. Most contests and sweepstakes rules prohibit mechanically reproduced entries.

9) Rules should state how often a person can enter a contest or sweepstakes. If a contestant can only enter once per person, then this should be clearly stated. "When I see this rule I will enter all my family and friends because I get as excited if one of them wins a prize as I do when I win," says Carol.

10) Rules should state if contestants can enter as often as they wish, and if this is allowed, must each entry be mailed separately.

11) Often the rules will call for an entry to be mailed in a standard number10 size envelope because some national sweepstakes envelopes are opened mechanically.

12) Rules may state that a day and evening telephone number be given. If the entry request an e-mail address and you don't own a computer, write "none" on that line. Same applies if you don't have a telephone. Never leave a line blank.

"I found that contests, sweepstakes, and promotions are strictly regulated and the laws vary from state to state with each state having its own registration requirements for sponsors," explains Carol.

"For example, in the official rules of a contest or sweepstakes a sponsor can use the word "void" in Florida, New York, and Rhode Island. This is because Florida and New York require a sponsor to register and post a bond if a prize exceeds $5,000. Rhode Island requires a registration if a prize amounts to $500 or more. If the rules of a contest or sweepstakes mention states where residents can't enter this can be good news for contestants living in other states because this means there will be that many fewer entries."

If a contest or sweepstakes is not legal where you live, Carol urges against writing to the sponsor, but recommends writing the legislature of that state to agitate for contest-law reform. "There's a reason for the regulations... mostly for the prevention of fraud and abuse. Regulations prevent the families and friends of people who work for the sponsors from entering contests or sweepstakes because these people might have insider information that could help them win."

"Many sponsors will hire independent firms to judge contests and pick sweepstakes winners because this takes the responsibility off the company that is sponsoring a contest or sweepstakes," Carol says.

Despite the possibility of winning big in a contest or sweepstakes, Carol reminds any would-be participant that it isn't all fun and games: "There is the liability of having to pay taxes on winnings because they count as income and must be declared on income tax returns in the United States, while prizes are normally tax-exempt in Canada," she says, "I won't enter a contest or sweepstakes unless I know I can afford to pay the taxes on the prize."

In Carol's thesis, she advises prize-winners to hire a good accountant to sort out their taxes: "Don found an accountant who advised us to keep records and receipts and tally up all my contesting and sweepstakes expenses, such as money spent on postage stamps, paper, envelopes, pencils, pens, markers, index cards, stickers, address labels, paper clips, dictionaries, books on contesting, subscriptions to contesting newsletters, etc. The supplies can add up in a year and by keeping a total it can help to defray some of the tax liability."

23

When Carol saw an article in the paper stating that the Drama Department at Washington University was sponsoring a "Write a Play" contest as part of their annual playwright festival, she knew this was her chance to knock another goal off her "Dream List," "TO WRITE A PLAY."

"I wrote my one act play as a romantic comedy based on an event that happened to my mother-in-law, Mabel Shaffer," says Carol, "When Mabel was 72 her former high school beau, Chester Hungate, called her from his home in Huntington, West Virginia. He told her he was a widower and had recently read in their hometown newspaper that she was a widow. After several more telephone conversations Chester asked if he could come to Columbia and visit her. Mabel agreed and I was able to observe the romance as it was rekindled. Mabel was excited, giddy and nervous as a schoolgirl. She worried that Chester wouldn't find her attractive anymore; worried that he would be disappointed. Some of her lady friends were jealous that she had a gentleman friend, and her daughter didn't approve that Chester and her Mom had hit it off. As I wrote my play, I tried to describe all the emotions as they'd actually unfolded. I titled the play "The Phone Call" because it opens with the telephone ringing, and Mabel getting the call from Chester."

Carol didn't win the playwright contest, but that didn't stop the play she wrote from making its way to a stage. The Columbia Woman's Club was hosting a variety show, and Carol offered them her one-act play. They pulled it off without a hitch. *"The Phone Call* was a huge success, and the audience laughed at all the proper places!" She says.

"Columbia Woman's Club also helped me to check off goal number three on my "Dream List".... "HAVE MY OWN NEWSPAPER COLUMN," says Carol. "As the recording secretary for the club, one of my duties was to write and submit articles about the club's activities for the local newspaper. One day after I had submitted an article the Editor of the newspaper asked if I would be interested in writing a column for his paper. He explained I would have a byline and my photo would be printed next to the column. I seized the opportunity and agreed to his job offer. I loved writing the column and the extra money came in handy as well!"

"I didn't have a lot of extra time," says Carol, "but I learned to utilize what spare time I did have for entering contests or sweepstakes. If we had a stand at a craft fair, or if I had a doctor or dentist appointment or anywhere that I might have to wait, I'd bring entry forms to fill out. Sometimes people in a waiting room would watch me and ask what I was doing. When I'd tell them that I was filling out entry blanks for a contest or a sweepstakes, they'd invariably say: 'Oh, I don't bother... nobody wins those things' or "I'm not lucky."

"I tell the doubters I meet that if they would rid themselves of their negative thinking they might win. I like to quote Norman Vincent Peale, the champion of positive thinking and author of the book, "The Power of Positive Thinking" who wrote, 'Your unconscious mind has a power that turns wishes into realities. Faith in yourself makes good things happen and you develop the power to reach goals." This is so true! When I enter a contest or sweepstakes I think positive...I expect to win. I believe that the most important step toward succeeding at anything is to believe you will succeed...that you will be successful."

After Carol had graduated from college, she decided to turn her passion for contesting up a notch. "I was eager to see just how far and what I could accomplish with my hobby by utilizing all the information I had gleaned from the research I'd done for my college paper," she says. "As a result I've found an avocation I thoroughly enjoy and in that time frame, I have managed to win over $200,000 in prizes (for myself, family, and friends), and have had more fun and adventure than I thought I'd ever have."

The first thing Carol did as a serious "contesting" enthusiast was to get organized. She set up a workplace in the extra bedroom of her house. "The workplace provided a quiet, orderly place where I could concentrate as I filled out entry blanks and/or post cards, decorated entries, wrote essays, etc."

Some examples of the supplies Carol has in her desk:
1) An assortment of colored pens, pencils, and markers.
2) Plain white number10 standard size envelopes and plain white stationery.
3) Colorful envelopes. Contact card and stationery stores and ask if they have any surplus envelopes or stationery they'd like to get rid of.
4) An assortment of colorful interesting stickers.
5) Colorful stationery with flowers, animals, balloons, or interesting designs on them.
6) Plain white and brightly colored 3" by 5" index cards.
7) Supply of post cards from the post office.
8) Picture post cards.
9) Assortment of colorful bingo dabbers.
10) Magnifying glass...helpful for reading the fine print!
11) Pinking sewing shears.
12) Variety of stamps.
13) Assortment of rubber stamps.
14) Shoe box. Keep duplicate entry blanks in a shoe box in a bottom drawer of the desk.

As Carol points out, "Many hobbies, like golfing or stamp collecting, can be expensive, but contesting is relatively inexpensive. It's a hobby anyone can do...men and women, old people, children, shut-ins, even handicapped people. You don't have to be a rocket scientist, but a little creativity does help!"

24

Once Carol had her working area organized, she put on her thinking cap to come up with some effective strategies for winning sweepstakes: "Up to this time I had concentrated primarily on winning contests. Now that I was organized, and had an arsenal of information about contests, promotions, and sweepstakes from the research I had done for my college paper, I felt compelled to come up with special techniques for winning sweepstakes."

According to Carol, sweepstakes are more popular than contests because the people who enter don't have to do anything. Sponsors prefer sweepstakes as well because they don't have to spend time judging entries...a winner is determined with a random drawing.

Despite the random nature of winning a sweepstakes, Carol has developed a few gimmicks that help increase the odds of winning:

1) Print name, address, and telephone number on an entry with a bright magic marker and use the marker to address the envelope that the entry will be mailed in. Address post cards with a bright marker.

2) Draw a picture on an entry to reflect the prize. Carol explains how this tactic has proven fruitful on one particular occasion: "When the Upper Deck Baseball Card company sponsored a sweepstakes with the prize being the opportunity to be the 'Honorary Manager' for the 1964 St. Louis Cardinals Baseball Team in an 'Old-Timers' game at Busch Stadium in St. Louis against the 1964 New York Yankees... entered all the men in my family. My strategy was to draw a bright red Cardinal bird on the entry blanks. Donald won, but wasn't able

to attend The Upper Deck Card Company allowed him to transfer the prize to his Dad, which was unusual because most often a prize is not transferable"

3) If a sweepstakes rules call for a post card, use a picture post card for appeal rather than a standard post card from the post office. "Whenever I travel, I purchase colorful, eye-catching picture post cards for use in future sweepstakes since picture post cards are usually the size stipulated in sweepstakes rules."

Carol asserts that contesting is one area of life where following the rules always pays off, and has repeatedly allowed her to check off even more spots on her 'Dream List'.

"When chAnnl 5 KSDK-TV television station in St. Louis sponsored a "Day With Oprah" sweepstakes to win a trip to Chicago I knew this was a sweepstakes I had to win," says Carol, "I am a big fan of Oprah and very much wanted to meet her. In fact, I had written "MEET OPRAH" on my "Dream List". If I won the sweepstakes I would be able to check off Goal number10."

"The picture post card strategy worked and I won the sweepstakes! I sent a postcard of Chicago as Harpo Studios where Oprah tapes her show is located there. My prize package (for two) included airfare to Chicago, a limousine ride from the airport to Harpo Studios, a tour of the studio, a bag of Oprah goodies, and a delicious lunch at the posh Drake Hotel. The difficult part of this sweepstakes was in deciding who to take with me! Donna and Diana both wanted to go – Diana's name was picked from a hat."

Carol describes Oprah as "warm, friendly, and down to earth, both on and off camera."

"We discussed diets and she talked about how she's always on the go," says Carol, "We talked about my contesting hobby and she said she was impressed. Oprah is one great lady!"

4) For a "drop an entry into a box" sweepstakes, give an entry blank extra body by crumbling the entry or fan folding it before dropping it into a bin. "The first big prize I won by entering sweepstakes with an organized approach was a $10,000 Shopping Spree at the upscale Plaza Frontenac Mall in St. Louis," says Carol, "I carefully filled out an entry blank and crumbled it up before dropping it into the box. I hoped this strategy would enhance my odds of winning."

"I was given a pretty shopping bag filled with colored tissue paper and stuffed with gift certificates totaling $10,000 in denominations of $50 and $100 amounts," says Carol, "I asked if I could share the certificates with my family, and was told I could give them to whomever I wished. I gave certificates in the amount of $1,000 each to Don, our children, my sister, and mother. I encouraged them to purchase something special....something they'd dreamed of owning but couldn't afford. Winning a $10,000 Shopping spree is certainly any woman's dream and it happened to me...thanks to contesting!"

5) Wet an entry in water so it will be stiff (after it dries) so that the entry will more likely be picked out of a bin. If time allows, soak an entry blank in water that has been colored with food coloring to make the entry stiff and colorful.

"This strategy worked to win a 'Dinner with Rams Football Players' sweepstakes sponsored by Tostitos Pizza Company," explains Carol. "I took some entries home to wet them in water to make them stiff in an effort to enhance the odds of winning the sweepstakes. After the entries were dry I filled them out and returned the stiff blanks to the store and I dropped them into an entry box. About two weeks later I was notified that I had won the dinner which was held at Ozzie Smith's (retired St. Louis Cardinals baseball short stop) Restaurant. Ozzie Smith served as the host for the dinner with football players Marshal Faulk, Ram's Running Back, and Trent Green, Ram's injured Quarterback. After the dinner I played a football video game on a big screen television at the restaurant with Mr. Faulk. He sacked my quarterback twice. He and Mr. Green are perfect gentlemen and both autographed footballs for my grandsons."

6) Try pinking the edges of a sweepstakes entry to give the blank an unusual feel in the bin. Lamination works too.

7) Stick a colorful, eye-catching sticker on an entry blank or post card, preferably a sticker that reflects the prize offered in the sweepstakes.

8) Use a colored or homemade envelope for mailing an entry, unless the sweepstakes rules specifically call for a standard size number10 envelopes.

9) Stick all one-cent stamps on a large envelope so the envelope will "stand out and be noticed. "I used this technique for a "mail-in" sweepstakes with the prize being a Ram's Superbowl Party," says Carol, "Donald is an avid Rams football fan so he was thrilled when he was informed that he'd won the party. He and his friends had a great time enjoying an array of delicious foods as they watched the St. Louis Rams Football Team win the Superbowl!"

10) Spray a mail-in entry with cheap perfume so that when the envelope is opened a noticeable fragrance will draw attention to the entry. "It doesn't have to be expensive perfume.... I use the cheapest perfume I can find, but it works," Carol vouches.

11) Decorate an entry and/or the envelope with a colorful bingo dabber.

12) Glue a picture from a magazine onto an entry that reflects the prize offered.

"I had always wanted to visit San Francisco, so when I saw a sweepstakes with the prize being a trip to the 'City by the Bay' I was interested," Carol says, "To enhance my chances of winning I glued a picture of the Golden Gate

Winning Big

Bridge to one of my entries. It was over a year before I received a congratulatory letter that I had won the trip."

13) Decorate an entry or envelope with a rubber stamp.

"I first won a prize this way after I entered my family in a sweepstakes to win four tickets to see the Ringling Brothers Circus," says Carol, "I stamped several entries with colorful circus animals and my daughter-in-law, Debbie, won the tickets. She treated her mother, Sandy, and sons, David and Drew, to a wonderful night at the circus."

14) If the sweepstakes rules allow a 3 x 5 inch index card to be used as an entry blank, mail a brightly colored index card.

15) Use the label of the product of the company that is sponsoring a sweepstakes as an entry blank (unless rules state otherwise). Print pertinent information asked such as name, address and telephone number on the back of the label. Another strategy is to stick the product label from the sponsor's product on an entry blank. Both techniques will show the sponsors that you use their product.

"I used the label from a can of Fancy Fest Cat Food as an entry for a sweepstakes sponsored by the pet food company to win a gift certificate for "Fancy Fest" cat food. I used a Dole Pineapple label as an entry blank and Donna won a $100 gift certificate for the Discovery ChAnnl Store. I stuck a Chiquita sticker I'd peeled off bananas I bought, for a sweepstakes that won Donald an underwater camera."

16.) To win tickets to a concert, a Broadway play, or a movie give an entry a theatrical look by lightly brushing the entry with watered down glue and then sprinkle with glitter.

As you can see, once you get the hang of it, entering sweepstakes can be a lucrative hobby. I don't win every sweepstakes I enter, but I do win a high percentage of them and this is what keeps me going trying to come up with new creative ways for Winning Big!

25

After multiple victories in her contesting career, Carol had knocked quite a few items off her 'Dream List'.

It started out looking like this:

1.) GO BACK TO COLLEGE
2.) WRITE A PLAY
3.) HAVE MY OWN NEWSPAPER COLUMN
4.) VISIT LAS VEGAS
5.) SEE THE GRAND CANYON
6.) WORK IN A HOLLYWOOD MOVIE
7.) TAP DANCE ONE MORE TIME
8.) SEE A WHALE IN ITS NATURAL HABITAT
9.) DO A TELEVISION COMMERCIAL
10.) MEET OPRAH
11.) WRITE A BOOK
12.) BE A CONTESTANT ON A GAME SHOW
13.) CLIMB THE GREAT WALL OF CHINA
14.) ATTEND THE OLYMPIC GAMES
15.) TRAVEL THE WORLD
16.) KISS THE BLARNEY STONE AND SLEEP IN A CASTLE IN IRELAND
17.) MEET JACK BUCK
18.) BE ON THE RADIO
19.) CRUISE THE SOUTH PACIFIC
20.) VISIT NIAGARA FALLS

"I believe everyone should have a 'Dream List' of what they want to do and I strongly encourage young people to make such a list," says Carol. "I tell them their list will be different from everyone else because people have different interests, but the important thing is have a list. I tell them to think how sad it would be to wake up *old* one day with a lot of regrets that they hadn't done the things they had very much wanted to do in life." This is a life lesson that Carol took to heart after seeing it reflected in the experiences of her son, Donald.

When Donald turned 21 he was surprised with a special birthday telephone call from his childhood friend Bhrett Steppig, also known as "Moose."

"The day that Moose called Donald to wish him a "Happy 21st Birthday" he said he was living in Salt Lake City, Utah and training to be a professional firefighter," says Carol, "As young boys they had dreamed of growing up to be firefighters. Moose's telephone call had a profound effect on Donald. He'd forgotten their dream to be firefighters when they grew up. It looked like Moose would make it happen."

The phone call convinced Donald to pursue another career path. While he was still attending college and was close to earning a business degree, he was going to transfer his major and get a fire science degree.

Around the same time, Don Sr. retired after working for the Federal Government for 33 years. According to his wife, he had mixed feelings about retiring.

Although Carol enjoyed getting out shopping or pursuing projects and goals, she says her husband tended to prefer to stay home and watch TV while smoking cigarettes. The two had few shared interests and were drifting apart.

In August 1992, Carol heard of a contest that would allow her to fulfill another item on her 'Dream List'. If she won, she could be an extra in the Hollywood movie, *King of the Hill*."

Says Carol, "When I was notified that I'd been chosen I was absolutely thrilled!"

The movie, *King of the Hill,* is based on the memoirs of A.E. Hotchner, a famous writer who grew up in St. Louis during the Depression of the late 20's and early 30's. Carol appeared in eight scenes and wore two different costumes, working twelve hour days that began at five in the morning.

"Each day after wardrobe and make-up, the extras were asked to line up for the day's assignment. Dressed in period clothing and make-up we blended into the background during filming and I was impressed with how authentic were the costumes and settings," she says of the experience.

"I was impressed by the large variety of people from all walks of life working as extras," Carol recounts, "I met a racetrack official, a medical doctor, a machinist, a radio announcer, housewives, and teachers. They all said they hadn't agree to work in the move for the money, but wanted to work as an extra because they loved movies and wanted to see how a movie is made. The oldest extra was 92 years and old and the make-up artist didn't have to use any make-up on him."

"Some of the actors and extras complained about the long hours of waiting between scenes, but I soaked up every minute," she says, "I was paid scale for my work, but it was a job I would gladly have done for nothing. Being in a Hollywood movie was an adventure I'll never forget!"

Several months after shooting wrapped up, Carol received a letter in the mail inviting her and a guest to the premier in downtown St. Louis. Her contest victories has taken her on trips all around the world, but the experience awaiting her was something money couldn't buy.

"It was a pleasant surprise when I received an invitation in the mail inviting me and a guest to attend the premier...The premiere at the Shady Oak Theatre in Clayton, Missouri, was much like I imagined a movie premiere would be with lots of glitz...beautiful dresses and jewelry, men in tuxedos, limousines ...Donna went with me. I wore the sapphire blue sequined dress and diamond rings I had purchased with my $10,000 Shopping Spree and Donna wore the sequined black dress I had purchased with the shopping spree," she recounts, "Boy, did we glitter! When I purchased the dresses I wondered where in the world would I ever wear them, and then I got to wear a sequined dress to the "Old Timers Dinner and Reception" at Lou Brock's Restaurant, and now to a movie premiere. Donna and I drove to the event in the car Don had won. It was living a fantasy!"

Carol continued to enter contests wherever she found them, regardless of the prize offered. She even entered contests if nobody else did:

"When I saw an 'Oxymoron Contest' advertised in the (newspaper) inviting readers to submit a favorite oxymoron, Don, Donald, and I all thought it would be fun to enter the contest," she says.

"What a surprise when the paper came out and Don's oxymoron, ("Accurate Estimate") won first place, Donald's oxymoron, ("Pretty Ugly") won second place, and my oxymoron, ("Jumbo Shrimp") was third. We wondered if anyone else had entered. I found it amazing that all of us were allowed to win, since I knew that most contests and sweepstakes rules limit only one prize per family or household."

Carol finds many of the contests and sweepstakes she enters in the newspaper and magazines, but there are many other sources as well. Radio and television stations often advertise contests and sweepstakes.

"I will look for posters that are displayed in store windows, or posters that are hung in stores," she says, "Sometimes a business will display a bAnnr on the side of their building. One day while driving down a highway I saw a huge bAnnr displayed on the side of a Service Merchandise Store advertising a 'His and Hers Watches' sweepstakes. I turned my car around and went to the store so I could enter all my family in the sweepstakes. Donna and her husband Jim each won a watch."

Another method Carol recommends to spot contests and sweepstakes is to watch for a new chain-store opening, "because the new opening if often promoted with a contest or sweepstakes. I try to enter in as many of the area stores as possible, and if prizes are being given away at each store it is often possible to win in more than one store. This has happened to me several times."

Carol has realized over the years that in addition to winning prizes in contests, it is possible to benefit a little on the side as well:

"If I win a trip I make sure to sign up for frequent flier miles with the airline that I am flying with, and as a result I have been able to accumulate thousands of frequent flyer miles. This is like winning another trip!"

Carol's appearance in *King of the Hill* also created new opportunities.

Because she had worked as an extra in the movie, her name is now in the data base of a local casting director who casts extras for movies that are filmed in St. Louis.

When the made for TV movie *A Will of Her Own* was filmed in St. Louis, Carol got a call to appear as an extra. In 2006, she got a call to work in the movie *The Beauty and Apocalypse*, filmed in Waterloo, Illinois.

The summer of 1994, Don had a heart attack. Donald, an emergency medical technician at the time, rode along in the ambulance while Carol followed in a car. Though he survived, it was determined that Don had blockage in his arteries and needed a quintuple-by-pass. The doctor insisted that Don quit smoking.

"Don came home from the hospital weak and depressed and I quit writing my newspaper column so I could care for him. It was frustrating because I felt nothing I did pleased him," says Carol. Though Don survived, he was too weak to attend his son's college graduation ceremony with the rest of the family, when Donald graduated with dual business and fire science degrees.

That same year, Mark Richardson, Diana's husband, won a $2,000 air hockey table in a mail-in Coca-Cola sweepstakes that Carol had thoughtfully entered her son-in-law in. He also won a night at the Casino Queen Hotel in St. Louis in the KMOV-TV (CBS) Internet Sweepstakes. Mark's favorite win though was doing the play-by-play announcing for a televised St. Louis Blues hockey game – a prize from KMOX Radio mail-in postcard sweepstakes.

26

"I have always been a dreamer and have encouraged my children to follow their dreams as well," says Carol, "So I was pleased that Donald had chosen to follow his dream of becoming a professional firefighter. As David Jordon said,

"The world stands aside to let anyone pass who knows where he is going."

Despite fierce competition fighting for any firefighting position available, Donald soon found an opening in nearby St. Peters, Missouri, beating out four hundred other applicants. Within months, he had an apartment near his new job and was engaged to his longtime girlfriend, Debbie.

All, however, was not well at home. Since retiring, Don had become more and more reluctant to give Carol any discretionary money. One of his favorite quotes was,

"I believe in the Golden Rule. He who makes the gold sets the rules." Don controlled the purse strings.

"I resorted to some rather sneaky tactics when I needed money for something special such as new make-up or to go to a movie," she says, "Whenever we'd go grocery shopping I would purposely put expensive food items (like coffee, shortening, and olives) in the grocery cart. That way, if I needed money for something later, I would return one of the grocery products for cash. I was also quite proficient at using coupons and mail-in rebates."

Despite these methods, Carol realized that she'd have to find her own source of income if she wanted to maintain a steady cash flow independent from contesting:

Winning Big

"A new Wal-Mart Store was opening less than five miles from my house," she says, "Donna and I decided we'd apply for jobs at the store to earn spending money. We told the man who interviewed us that we preferred to work evenings. Donna was attending college during the day pursuing an elementary teaching degree, and I wanted my days free so I could enter contests and sweepstakes and remain active with the Columbia Women's Club."

Carol and Donna both liked working for Wal-Mart. Carol started out work as a Greeter, welcoming customers to the store.

"It was fun to see friends and relatives; sometimes I would see someone I hadn't seen for twenty years or more. I've been invited to birthday parties, weddings, and anniversaries by customers and I go. One day a member of Columbia Woman's Club came into the store, and said: "You mean you went to college so you could work at Wal-Mart?"

I was fifty-five years old, an age when many people retire. I wasn't looking for a stressful career. I wanted a job that was fun and I'd found it!"

"Another aspect of the job I enjoy is the charity work I have been able to do on behalf of Children's Miracle Network. After customers shop I will ask them if they would like to donate to CMN. Many donate, again and again, and to date I have collected over $50,000 for the charity. I doubt I could raise this much money for a charity if I didn't work for Wal-Mart."

June of 1996 arrived and Donald and Debbie's wedding was fast approaching. "There was an exulting feeling of happiness and anticipation in the air," says Carol, "I took my mother to the same bridal shop where Debbie had purchased her wedding gown so she could get a dress to wear to the wedding. Mom chose a pretty blue and white dress, but when she tried the dress on she said: 'This is the dress I want to be buried in when I die.' I told her that was a silly thing to say, but her words sent a chill up my back and left me with a feeling of trepidation."

The week before the wedding, Wilma had a fall down the stairs and broke her hip. "Mom was sad that she wouldn't be able to attend Donald and Debbie's wedding, but we promised to take lots of pictures and tell her all about it," says Carol.

A nurse from St. Elizabeth's Hospital called to tell us that Mom had died from a blood clot in her lungs. She died in her sleep.

"Mom's death was totally unexpected, especially since her doctor had said she was doing fine," says Carol, "I was so upset I could hardly think. I felt like I was spiraling around like water going down a drain. Mom had to overcome so many challenges in life yet had always been my pillar of strength, my inspiration, my best friend...and now she was gone."

Carol remembers her mother as a woman who was kind hearted and tried to make her daughters feel good about themselves, despite her own low self-esteem. "We were loved without expecting anything in return," says Carol.

Her funeral was held on the Wednesday before Donald's wedding. "It seemed incongruous to be burying Mom the same week that Donald was getting married, in the dress she had planned to wear to the wedding," says Carol. "I was immensely sad, but decided to rejoice in her life and not wallow in mourning over her death. I felt the best way to honor Mom would be to live the rest of my life to the fullest."

Wilma's death wasn't the only tragedy to strike the family in the week leading up to the wedding. Donald and Debbie's new house needed a new roof. Donald and one a friend were going to handle the job themselves. The day after the funeral,

Donald was up on the roof of his house for 14 hours, in 98-degrees heat...squatting from 6:30 a.m. until about 8:00 p.m. When he started to feel a tingling sensation in his foot he didn't think anything of it and continued to work until the roof was completed. This would turn out to be a crucial mistake.

The next day, he couldn't walk. The day before the wedding, Donald fell in the yard and was taken to the emergency room. At the hospital Donald's prognosis was grim. He was told that he might have permanent neurological damage.

"Donald was devastated," says Carol, "He had worked hard to become a firefighter and his livelihood depended on his mobility. He was told he had a 50-50 chance of getting feeling back in his legs."

That night Donald attended the rehearsal dinner with a cane. Still, he fell three times, once in the parking lot of the restaurant into a pile of broken glass, cutting his hands.

The day of the wedding Donald got a wheelchair and his best man, Chris Grueinger pushed him in the chair. Donald managed to gingerly walk to the front of the church and stand for the wedding ceremony.

"It had been a very emotional week with a lot of lows and highs, and we had all had to get used to laughing and crying on the very same day," Carol remembers. "Despite Mom's death, Donald's paralysis, and other misfortunes, Donald and Debbie did say: "I do" and tied the knot."

A few days after the wedding Donald visited a specialist in St. Louis and was told he would walk again. Donald was suffering from a common injury, a compressed nerve that had swollen up and the only cure was to wait it out.

27

"With Donald married and on his own, it was just Don and I alone in the house," recalls Carol, "Don mostly sat watching TV while I went to work at Wal-Mart or pursued my contesting endeavours. Though I'd won him some prizes he seemed distant – we'd drifted apart and we didn't talk much."

Carol continued to enter her family in contests and sweepstakes and on occasion, more than one of them would win a prize. Carol recounts some of the contests she won for her family members, with prizes ranging from the exceptional to the everyday:

"We are a sports loving family," says Carol, "So I always try to enter sweepstakes that have anything to do with sports, and as a result we've won several tickets to St. Louis Cardinal's baseball games and Rams football games. When K-Mart Stores and Nabisco sponsored an in-store drawing with the prize being sports equipment I entered family members. Donald won a hockey stick and puck, Donna won a basketball, Ryan and Jimmy each won a baseball and bat set, and Jimmy won a Rawlings batting machine."

"One day while shopping at the Westfield Mall in South County, St. Louis I saw a sweepstakes drawing at a Gordon's Jewellery Store. The prize was a set of crystal wine glasses valued at $120. I stood there and entered all the women in the family. Debbie and I each won a set of beautiful crystal glasses."

"There's nothing like a free haircut," says Carol, "It makes you feel good. When Great Clips Hair Salons sponsored a sweepstakes with the prizes being free hair cuts I entered all the family. Donna, Jim, Amanda, Diana, Mark, Donald, and Debbie all won a free hair cut. We were probably the best groomed family in town that week. We've had many other multiple wins, but this should give you an idea what a fun hobby contesting can be for the whole family!"

Carol had only worked at Wal-Mart a short time when she was asked to do a television commercial for the company. She readily agreed, knowing that she would be able to check off GOAL number 9 "DO A TELEVISION COMMERCIAL" that was on her "Dream List." The commercial made her face even more recognizable to those in the Wal-Mart community.

Due to her contesting hobby, people were starting to recognize Carol at the grocery store, the dentist or doctor's office, and at Wal-Mart, Carol says, "They'd ask, 'How do you do it, how do you win all that stuff?' I thought, "maybe I ought to make a video about my strategies and techniques for winning contests and sweepstakes?"

"The only problem was I didn't know anyone who made videos," she says, "Then I remembered that one of the ladies in Columbia Woman's Club had a son, Adam Crosley, who had a business that specialized in making television commercials. I contacted Adam and proposed my idea for a "How To" video in which I'd reveal my secrets for winning contests and sweepstakes. He agreed to finance and produce the video as a project for his company, Reel Impact."

Carol filmed the video, and her instructional video, *Win Big,* was on sale within weeks. At the same time, Carol was planting the seeds of another adventure, this time at Wal-Mart: "One day I suggested to fellow Greeters at Wal-Mart that we all go on a trip together to England. It was a strange proposal, but five of the Greeters thought it was a great idea...that is if we could all get off work at the same time. I asked the store's manager and he said, 'Go for it...you ladies have a nice time. I'll find someone to cover your hours." I was glad I had thought of the trip because it gave us something to look forward to in the following year....something to talk about and be excited about!"

28

"After my *Win Big* video was released there was a lot of publicity," says Carol, "I did a string of live radio interviews from my home, some as far away as New Zealand, and this enabled me to check off GOAL number18..."BE ON THE RADIO" off my "Dream List". People I didn't know recognized me and they'd ask me questions about contesting. I got a big kick out of all the attention."

Around this time, Carol met a man while waiting for Donna to finish her shifts at Wal-Mart: "There was no reason for me to talk to him, but I did," she says, "Politics, sports, child-rearing...I enjoyed to talking with my new friend, and felt drawn to him like a moth to a flame."

"At first I thought he might be Jim Mundy," she says. "I hadn't seen Jim since I was seventeen, but the man was tall like Jim, very gregarious and funny, and seemed to have a lot of vitality. He was jovial and had the same hearty laugh that I remembered Jim as having. All through the fall and winter months I'd stay after work and talk with the man. Months went by before I learned his name was Edward Reinbold. He told me his friends called him Ed. He also told me he was divorced."

"My greeter friends and I fantasized about our trip to England the coming year," says Carol, "When I first started working at Wal-Mart I had signed up for the company's stock purchasing plan and had stock purchase deducted from my pay each payday. I planned to sell my stock to pay for the trip."

Springtime arrived, and Carol noticed that some of the greeters were becoming less enthusiastic about the impending trip to England. One by one, eventually all the women cancelled.

"I was very disappointed," she says, "I had never been to Europe and was very much looking forward to the trip. I told Ed that my friends had bailed out on the England trip. He was sympathetic...said he knew how I must feel. Out of the blue, and totally unplanned, I blurted the words, "Why don't we go to Europe? We could get separate rooms."

His jaw dropped into his lap. Stunned, he looked at me.

"You mean it?" he asked.

"Yes I do...I want to see Europe," I replied.

He said he'd always wanted to see Germany, Austria, and Switzerland and asked how I felt about going there. I said I didn't care which country we went to. I just wanted to go to Europe."

"Don was aware that I was planning a trip to England with fellow greeters, so I just let him assume that I was going with them," she says, "I was nervous and somewhat uncertain, but was still determined to go. I wanted to travel and see the world and I knew I would have to make it happen. When I got to the airport in St. Louis I saw Ed looked a little nervous too, but excited and ready to commence on a wonderful adventure."

"Ed was the perfect travel companion," recalls Carol, "He was enthusiastic, had a great sense of humor, and took photos everywhere we went. I kept a journal of what we saw, and took notes of all the facts that our tour guides told us."

Carol has fond memories of her trip to Europe, which included visits to the Bavaria region of Germany, the Austrian highlands and the Swiss Alps. The duo even managed to pay a visit to the tiny principality of Liechtenstein, one of the world's smallest countries. Along the way she got a chance to see life in a way most Americans are unaccustomed to, in a land of natural beauty and grandeur.

"I hated for our wonderful trip to Europe to be over," she says, "Europe was everything I had thought it would be, only more. I wanted to see more of Europe and knew I had to somehow find the way."

29

After arriving back home in St. Louis, Carol returned back to her normal routine.

"I returned home from Europe exhausted, but glad I had gone on the trip," says Carol, "I was glad to go back to work. I continued to see Ed when he came into the store and occasionally on my day off we'd go to the St. Louis Zoo and ride the zoo train or go to concerts in the park."

It was her newfound companionship with Ed that acted as the catalyst that would put an end to her now-stagnant marriage.

"One day we went to a park that overlooked the Mississippi River and Ed said that when he was a boy his grandparents lived near the park and they would bring him there so he could watch the Admiral Excursion Boat cruise by," Carol remembers.

"I told him I had worked on the *Admiral* and how my car had rolled into the river and hit a rudder of the boat. Ed had brought his camera and he asked some people at the park if they would take our picture. They took several, and he took some pictures of me by myself. When he had the film developed he had doubles made and gave me a set. I hid the photos in a bottom drawer of my dresser, thinking they would be safe there."

She was wrong.

"Don found the photos and confronted me. He asked me if there was anything he could do to save the marriage, but there really wasn't. I was unhappy and we had drifted apart and needed to end the relationship."

The divorce was finalized August 1999 and the two sold their house. Carol used her half of the money from the sale to buy a condo. Don ended up buying a small house in the town where he'd grown up. Today he is living happily in his old hometown.

"Christmas '99 looked like it might be bleak," says Carol, "Money was tight because of all the expenses I'd had getting settled. I had only been awarded 40% of Don's pension check because I was still young enough to work and I wasn't old enough to collect social security, but I did have my Wal-Mart salary. I worried how I'd come up with money for Christmas gifts and stamps for my Christmas cards. I had addressed 24 cards, but I didn't have any extra money for stamps to mail them. I didn't tell Ed or my children just how broke I was – and then, oddly enough, I found exactly 24 stamps in a parking lot and mailed my cards."

Carol also continued to see Ed, and he soon won the affection of her family as well. Over time, the two became very close, and involved in a serious relationship.

"Ed asked me to marry him, but I declined. I told him that after being under Don's thumb for 38 years I doubted that I would ever marry again," she says. "I was 58 and he was 63, marriage wasn't something I was striving for."

The two often reminisced about their time in Europe, and eventually, Carol entered Ed's name in a contest and he won a grand prize of $4,000 in a sweepstakes and they began planning another trip overseas.

"We used the money to book a tour to the capital cities of Scandinavian countries and St. Petersburg, Russia," says Carol, "The first city we visited on the tour was Copenhagen, Denmark, the capital of the oldest kingdom in the world and Scandinavia's largest and liveliest city."

Carol recounts her first days in the far northern region:

"We visited the old sailor's quarters and it was rich with pubs, boutiques, and old sailing ships. We saw the wistful "Little Mermaid," famous for greeting sailors as they come into the harbor at Copenhagen and for inspiring Hans Christian Anderson's fairy tale."

Ed and Carol next found themselves in the Norwegian city of Oslo, the 900-year old city founded by Viking warriors. Ironically, one location Carol remembers best is the key to one of the few contests she wouldn't be likely to win in her lifetime: "Our favorite place to visit at this beautiful city was the architecturally magnificent Oslo City Hall where the Nobel banquet and festivities take place each year in Oslo. We also saw the Peace Prize Headquarters where it is determined who the winner will be."

Soon they were on the way to Stockholm, Sweden, known as the "Venice of the North" for its canal's and waterways, and from there to Helsinki, Finland.

"What I love about traveling is I learn so much," says Carol, "I learned…Girls do better at getting into college (in Finland). As a result there are more women doctors, dentists, accountants, etc. But if there is a job opening, however, girls aren't hired as quickly as boys. Our guide told us that Finland is considerate of mothers. After a woman has a child she gets one year off work, but still receives 60% of her salary. She can stay home for up to three years and still be guaranteed her job when she returns, but will not be paid for the additional years away from work."

When Carol and Ed crossed the border to St. Petersburg, Russia, they were on the edge of their seats. Security was strict! "Our bus had to drive over a pit so guards could search under the bus," says Carol, "We were told that when soldiers came onto the bus and that we should not act silly or laugh, because the soldiers might think we were laughing at them. Three soldiers came aboard the bus and slowly walked up and down the aisle. Before leaving they stopped next to Ed and asking him to stand up. He refused, fearing they wanted to take him off the bus. The soldiers insisted until Ed finally stood up, and when he did, the soldiers asked him to take their photo with him. Ed agreed and I took a picture with my camera of Ed and the soldiers."

For Carol, one striking factor that put Russia apart from the Scandinavian nations was the crippling poverty: "There were poor people wherever we went," she says, "and they had creative ways to earn money. They never begged, but would try instead to make money by selling souvenirs, playing music at the entrance of various places we visited, or sometimes elderly ladies would try to sell their crocheted doilies."

Despite the poverty, Carol says that few cities in the world can match the grace of St. Petersburg, known as the "Window to the West." Peter the Great, ruler of Russia during the construction of the city, intended to make St. Petersburg a rival of Paris, France in wealth and grandeur. "When we got back to our hotel, we were told not to leave because there are many 'bandits' in Russia," says Carol.

"Ed and I felt we hadn't traveled all this way to just sit in a hotel, so we found an English-speaking driver who took us to what he referred to as 'The Black Market.' He told us there would be lots of shopping there, and that he would be come back in two hours to get us."

The two did a whirlpool of shopping, buying presents for the whole family. Still, an important item was missing and would have to be addressed before returning to the States.

"Donald collects uniform fire patches and I've managed to get patches at all the countries I've visited," says Carol. "I asked the taxi driver if he could take us to a fire station so I could get a Russian patch for Donald."

"Like firefighters everywhere, the Russian firemen

were hospitable and friendly," says Carol. "I gave the firemen fire patches from Donald's fire department and the fire captain ripped a patch off his uniform. He opened a desk drawer and gave me a Russian deck of cards, a book of matches, a calendar, photos of the fire station, and medallions. He even wrote Donald a letter...in Russian."

Carol returned from the trip exhausted, but ready to go again. It seemed that the more she traveled, the more she wanted to travel. "We couldn't get enough of traveling and seeing the world and constantly talked about where we would like to go next," she says. "I couldn't get over how much my life had changed. I was traveling and seeing places I'd only dreamed of visiting. I was living on my own, and making it... thanks in a big part to Ed."

"Being a contester is much like being a gambler," explains Carol. "When a gambler wins, his actions are reinforced and he tries to win again. The same is true for me. I became determined to win us another trip. I entered every sweepstakes I could find. Sometimes we wouldn't win the grand prize trip, but we'd often win something." Her efforts were successful when Ed's name was drawn for a Caribbean cruise. "I was determined one of us would win the cruise, and Ed did!"

30

The prize consisted of a seven-day cruise aboard the carnival cruise ship *Destiny*, at the time the largest cruise ship afloat. The ship made stops on the islands of St. Croix, St. Thomas, and in the Bahamas.

Ed was in awe of the experience," recalls Carol, "He said he felt like he'd died and gone to heaven. "As always we hated to see a trip come to an end and return to reality. The good news was that we were accumulating frequent flier miles and hoped that we would soon have enough miles for a free trip."

After returning home from the cruise, Ed and Carol decided to cohabitate, share expenses, and save the extra money for traveling. Ed gave up his apartment and moved in with Carol. It was a strategy that worked.

"The year after Ed moved in with me, he and I went on three trips," says Carol, "The first was a 22 day tour of Europe, made possible with frequent flier miles. It was as if we'd won another trip!"

Carol recounts her experiences in the United Kingdom:
"Our tour started with a visit to St. Paul's Cathedral, the church where Prince Charles and Princess Diana were married and where Winston Churchill's funeral was held. It has been a place of pilgrimage for nearly 1400 years...From the church we went to Buckingham Palace, home of Queen Elizabeth. Before going inside we saw the "Changing of the Guards." The palace has 600 rooms and all are in use, but Queen Elizabeth only uses twelve rooms."

"On the way to see the magnificent clock tower, Big Ben, we drove past Number Ten Downing Street, the Prime Minister of England's residence. Big Ben is really big... bigger than I had imagined, located next to the Houses of Parliament buildings. Not far from these buildings is the Westminster Abby Church where Princess Diana's funeral was held. Seeing all these famous landmarks made me feel like I was in an English fairytale."

According to Carol, Ed really enjoyed seeing London and said,
"I like what I've seen here so much that if I had to go home early, and not see the other countries, I wouldn't be too disappointed."

The traveling duo left London early the following morning and boarded a ferry for the Continent, taking the ferry to Belgium. The tour group was met by a new tour guide, a young Frenchman named Allen, who would be with Carol's group for the duration of the tour.

"The most important landmark we saw in Belgium was the Grand Palace, where King Leopold lived," says Carol. "We saw the Giant Atom, built in Brussels for the 1859 World's Fair."

"We were surprised when Allen told us that Brussels National Symbol is a little boy urinating. The boy is famous because he saved Brussels from burning by urinating on a lit match," she says, "You learn so much when you travel."

The group spent the night in Brussels and the next day traveled to The Netherlands, called the "low lands" because the area is below sea level. Carol visited several windmills and Allen explained that the Dutch people use windmills to dry out the water in fields and marshes and to reclaim the land from the sea. There is a famous story about a young lad who saved the country by sticking his thumb in a dike that had a hole that was leaking though Allen told the tour this was just a metaphor.

"We passed several coffee shops where the menu not only includes coffee, soda, and sandwiches, but also lists of (marijuana and hashish products) on the menu. A sign in the window of one of the coffee houses read,
"Why drink and drive if you can smoke and fly?"

Early the next morning, Carol and Ed embarked on a 300 mile ride through picturesque Rhineland areas of Germany. As they drove along the romantic Rhine River, they had a wonderful view of castles and vineyards along the riverbanks. As they travelled, they got to know their fellow travelers.

"The other travellers tried to guess what Ed had done for a living before retiring," Carol says. "With his flat top hair cut and 6 foot 3 frame the consensus was that he was a retired military officer. He wouldn't tell them what he'd done for a living, preferring to remain a man of mystery. Some of the travelers nicknamed him "General" and they weren't totally off because he had been a military policeman in the army. I knew he'd retired from a bank where he'd been an auditor, but I didn't tell the other travelers. It was more fun to keep them guessing."

After a trip through Germany and a return visit to Bavaria, Carol and Ed were once again in Austria, land of the mountains.

"It seemed we were forever crossing borders," comments Carol, "The next day we crossed a border into Italy. Once again we were in the Alps. I had forgotten how high they are! The scenery through the Brenner Pass was breathtaking."

All along the route, Carol was on the lookout for fire stations to gather patches for her son's collection, having picked up patches in the UK and Austria: "We stopped for a two hour lunch at Cortina, Italy where I asked the proprietor of the restaurant where the nearest fire station was located," says Carol. "He made a telephone call and before we knew what happened, a fire truck arrived at the restaurant to take Ed and me to the station. All the Italian firemen were nice and friendly even though many couldn't speak English. They exchanged patches then gave me a calendar of the station which all the men autographed. The fire chief prepared espresso coffee and the men served us sandwiches and cookies. After we ate the food Ed took pictures of the men by their fire truck. They were so cordial we could hardly get them to take us back to the bus."

After a brief drive, they arrived in the legendary city of Venice.

"Venice looks exactly like I imagined," says Carol. "There are no streets or cars in Venice, so everything must be done by boat. Boats bring goods to the stores. When people move, their furniture is put onto boats. Garbage is picked up by boats, and people go to church in a boat. We even saw a concrete mixer mixing concrete on a boat."

The second day (in Venice) we were on our own," she says. "We strolled through shops and looked for souvenirs, fed pigeons at Marc's Square, and then after dark we went back to see the city at night. It is even more beautiful at night because the buildings and bridges are illuminated with lights. I'm a terrible romantic, so being in romantic Venice with Ed, holding hands and laughing at silly things was pure heaven, and I felt twenty years old again. Reluctantly we left Venice. Ed said Venice is his favorite place he's ever been in the world and I agreed!"

It was a long drive southward to the next destination: Rome. The city that had been the hub of the ancient civilized world was now Europe's premier hub for tourism. Sights visited by Carol and Ed included the Vatican, the Sistine Chapel and St. Peters Basilica.

In the afternoon, they were scheduled to do a city tour of Rome. Carol couldn't believe it as we drove by the balcony were Mussolini had addressed the Italian people during his Fascist regime: "I was a little girl when it happened and now I was in Rome seeing the exact place it happened," she recalls, "It was too surreal."

The next day was "Arrivaderci Roma." The trip was half over, and as always, Carol felt that time went by too fast. The next destination was Pompeii, Italy. This ancient city was destroyed by the Mt. Vesuvius volcano.

"Pompeii is fascinating!" Carol says, "I had thought it was lava from the volcano that killed the people in 1600 B.C. but it was poisonous gas from the volcano that actually killed them. The city was then covered by volcanic ashes and this is what preserved the city for hundreds of years until an excavation was started in 1748."

Winning Big

31

The tour continued its winding path down the Italian peninsula, visiting cities of culture stretching from Antiquity to the Renaissance.

"I was anxious to get to Pisa, Italy," she says, "I have always been fascinated with pictures I've seen of the famous Leaning Tower of Pisa, and now I was actually going to get to see it...Pisa was the home of Galileo and it was on the Leaning Tower that he proved that there is gravity on earth by dropping objects from the top of the tower. As we climbed the stairs to get to the top I couldn't help but visualize Galileo as he climbed the very same stairs."

From Pisa, the tour group moved north, through Genoa and into the French Riviera, before stopping for the night in Nice.
Soon after arriving in France, the tour was taken to the pocket-sized principality of Monaco, at the time ruled by Prince Rainer and Princess Grace, formerly an American actress. According to Carol, "The country is so beautiful it looks like a movie set."

"(In Monaco), we visited the exclusive ritzy Monte Carlo Casino where the international jet-set like to play," says Carol. "We weren't allowed to go inside and gamble at the legendary casino because we were dressed casually, but we were allowed to peek inside and see what it looked like. It is very beautiful and elegant! In front of the casino there was row after row of expensive luxury cars."

For the next few days, Carol and Ed visited various French cities as the tour made its way to Paris, France. "As we traveled along the same route Napoleon had traveled, we saw some of France's most unspoiled scenery, especially the vineyard regions that provide France's renowned wines," Carol says. "When we finally arrived at Paris it was dusk, but we could see the famous Eiffel Tower in the distance."

The tour's first stop in Paris was the famed Louve, where they observed various art treasures, among them The Mona Lisa, The Dying Slave, the Venus de Milo, and The Winged Victory.

"The next day our Parisian immersion included a panoramic city tour," says Carol. "We got to see many of the best known Parisian sights: La Sorbonne, Arc de Triumph, a gold statue of Joan of Arc, a drive down Sycamore-lined fashionable Champs Elysees, a walk through Luxembourg, and a photo stop for Paris' most enduring symbol, The Eiffel Tower."

They went to the Notre Dame Cathedral and viewed gargoyles and religious icons from the Gothic era. "The inside of the church is even more beautiful than the outside," she says. "I found it difficult to believe that such a gorgeous church had at one time been used as a stable for horses. Paris is a walking town and for the rest of the day Ed and I walked our legs off, but like true Parisians, we took time for conversation and coffee at a sidewalk cafe. We found the city to be sheer magic."

"Allen told us that during the Second World War, Hitler wanted Paris destroyed (to prevent it from falling into Allied hands). The German General in charge had bombs placed under monuments, but when he met with Hitler and saw how crazy Hitler was, the general decided not to detonate the bombs."

But all good things come to an end. "Much to our dismay our trip was over, and it was time to return home," Carol recalls, "During the flight Ed asked me if I'd ever like to go back to Europe again someday.
"You betcha," I replied, without any hesitation!"

32

Not long after returning home from Europe, Carol was victorious in another contest, a sweepstakes she'd entered at the last minute before going on her last trip abroad. The prize was another trip, this time to San Diego on the Pacific coast.

"Ed and I loved San Diego," says Carol, "We had such a fun time in San Diego that we hated it when our stay was over and it was time to go home."

Carol was about to get another kind of opportunity as well: "After we returned home from San Diego I received a telephone call invitation inviting me to attend a "time-share" promotion. The caller stated that if I and a guest would agree to attend a time-share promotion we would receive two airline tickets to Las Vegas and accommodations at Harrah's Casino on the Las Vegas Strip."

"We had a ball in Las Vegas!" She says. "We liked all the bright neon lights and loved visiting the casinos... Our favorite casino was The Venetian which is mirrored after Renaissance Venice. The Venetian has gone to extraordinary lengths to authentically recreate Marc's Square, graceful arched bridges over flowing canals where we enjoyed a relaxing gondola boat ride, colorful piazzas, and stone walkways."

During the flight home from Las Vegas, the happy couple talked about what a fantastic year of travel 1999 had been and wondered what the year 2000 would bring. Neither had visited Alaska, and ended up booking a cruise to the far north for May, 2000. In their travels all over the world, Ed and Carol had grown close in a short amount of time. He had reinvigorated her life.

"I was glad that Ed and I had met," says Carol. "When we were together I was happy and vibrant... felt very much alive. He made me realize that no matter how old I got, I still had the potential for happiness in love. He made me feel confident that I could do anything that I set my mind to He inspired me, encouraged me, and made me feel good about myself."

Carol became aware of the "2000 Ms. Illinois Senior American Classic Women's Pageant". The pageant wasn't a beauty contest, but rather a competition to prove that life is still fun and exciting for seniors. The contest caught Carol's eye. She recounts Ed's reaction upon discovering his significant other was competing in the pageant:

"A pageant would be a different kind of challenge for me, so I sent for an application. When I told Ed I was entering the pageant he said,
"You're entering what?"
Even though I had won trips and prizes, he didn't fully understand contesting. I had been entering contests and sweepstakes practically all my life and I knew the odds... knew how to enhance my chances of winning. Even with all the prizes that I'd won as proof, he'd say,
"You'll never win."
I'd just wink and say,
"It doesn't matter if I win or not, it's the excitement of the chase that keeps me going," Then I'd tell him,
"I'm not afraid of failure because as far as I'm concerned failure only proves I've tried". Laughing he'd say,
"You know, you have no shame!"
He may not have understood what contesting was about, but he was supportive in my undertakings, and though he may not have thought I'd win, he always hoped I would."

Carol worked hard to gain the support of Columbia's business community, convincing many merchants and professionals to sponsor her bid in the pageant. She needed money for a gown and for travel expenses, but got so much financial support that her daughters could accompany her to the pageant itself. Since she had finished college when she was in her 50s, Carol opted to make "Continuing Education for seniors" her platform at the pageant.

The pageant was a three-day affair and there were three categories for judging the contestants: an evening gown presentation, a three minute talent competition, and answering questions submitted by judges. Carol made her own gown and choreographed a tap dance routine to Gene Kelly's 'Singing in the Rain' for the talent segment. "I hoped to gain a leg up on the competition by choosing a talent that takes a lot of energy and stamina... proving that I was one senior who had (real spirit)," she says, "Also, by doing a tap routine I would be able to check GOAL number 7 off my Dream List : "TAP DANCE ONE MORE TIME IN PUBLIC."

Carol didn't win the Ms. Illinois Senior title, according to one of the judges, because she did not belong to any senior citizen organizations. She did, however, win the talent competition. Carol's contesting tenacity went a long way towards her success in the pageant.

"After I returned home from my participation in the pageant, Ed and I saw an ad in the Sunday newspaper advertising a special three day trip to Los Angeles, California. We figured this would be enough time for a quick tour of Hollywood."

33

For Carol and Ed, the trip to Los Angeles was too good of a deal to pass up, "and as Mark Twain once wrote, "Twenty years from now you will be more disappointed by the things that you didn't do than by the ones you did do. So throw off the bowlines. Sail away from the safe harbor. Catch the trade winds in your sails. Explore. Dream. Discover," says Carol," Ed and I were taking his advice. You might say we'd become traveling fools!"

"We crammed a lot of activity into the three days we spent in Los Angeles. The (time) flew by and it was soon time to return home. Since Ed and I are both big movie buffs, we found it to be a wonderful experience getting to visit the movie capital of the world."

After returning home from Los Angeles there was no time for a hiatus. It would soon be time for Ed and Carol to leave on their Alaskan Cruise, booked the previous year. "I barely had time to get our clothes washed!" She says.

They had chosen an Alaskan Cruise tour package that included visits to cities in the U.S. and British Columbia, and flew to San Francisco to start the trip. The travelers toured the city before continuing their voyage north.

"The next day we drove up the coast through the state of Oregon," says Carol. "Our next rest stop was at Eugene, Oregon's capital. We crossed the Columbia River to Washington, where we could see Mount St. Helens in the distance."

"As we approached Seattle, Washington we could see the city's pretty skyline with the recognizable Needle Restaurant. Ed and I agreed that the trip had been most enjoyable so far and we were looking forward to our cruise and getting to see Alaska," she says, "We arrived at Vancouver, British Columbia, where we enjoyed a tour of the beautiful cosmopolitan city before boarding the cruise ship."

Carol and Ed boarded a Holland Cruise Ship for the cruise to Alaska. The first port of call was downtown Juneau, Alaska's capitol city: "As soon as Ed and I debarked from the ship we boarded a tramcar for an exhilarating ride from sea level up through the Southeast Alaska Rain Forest." Experiencing the vast forestry and natural beauty of Alaska, for Carol, was simply breathtaking.

The next port of call was Skagway, Alaska, gateway city to the Klondike Gold Fields. The next day the ship stopped at Glacier National Park where, in Carol's words, "the grandeur of Alaska thrilled and delighted us beyond expectation."

"We had seven glorious days on our cruise. We even enjoyed the days at sea, but then it was over," recounts Carol, "The day the ship docked it was a gloomy, rainy morning as we boarded a waiting tour bus for the last leg of our trip." They visited several small towns and villages in the Pacific Northwest region along their route.

"As we drove through British Columbia the scenery was beautiful," Carol says, "As we sat on the bus gazing out the window, Ed and I soaked up as much of the beauty of the scenery as we could, but Sometimes I'd give in and have a short nap with my head resting on his shoulder."

The tour bus made its way throughout the region rolling through Idaho, Montana and Utah before coming to an end in Salt Lake City, where the wary travelers boarded a flight back to Illinois.

They were finally going home.

34

"Because Ed and I were older when we met, we felt an urgency to see and do everything we possibly could," explains Carol, "So we went on one more trip in the year 2000... Thanks to all the frequent flier miles we had accumulated from our trips to San Diego, Las Vegas, Los Angeles, and Alaska we had enough miles to qualify for a free domestic trip. This was like winning a trip!"

They decided to "VISIT NIAGARA FALLS" ...GOAL number 20 on Carol's Dream List, and went there in September of 2000.

In between trips abroad and around the country, Carol never forgot that, apart from her passion for travel, she was dedicated to contesting. In a case of Déjà vu, A producer for *To Tell the Truth* called Carol and asked if she would be interested in being a contestant on the new, revised version of the show. Carol agreed.

Subsequently, she appeared on the show after she and Ed returned from Niagara Falls. "I very much appreciated Ed going with me to the taping," she says, "He sat in the front row of the studio audience, smiling and clapping, and very supportive. His presence helped me to stay calm as I participated in the nationally televised game show, and I was able to stump a celebrity panel and the studio audience and check off goal number 12 on my Dream List to "BE A CONTESTANT ON A GAME SHOW."

"After we returned home from the taping, Ed decided to purchase a computer," says Carol. "This opened a whole new world for me of entering contests and sweepstakes on the Internet and Ed enjoyed sending e-mails and doing research on the computer."

The possibilities presented by the Internet blew Carol away. With page after page of contests and sweepstakes promotions, the veteran contester was in heaven. With on-line "portals" designed to lead to certain linked sites, Carol was able to maximize her contesting potential. "A site I found particularly interesting was iWon.com," says Carol. "Would-be winners have to register in order to have a chance to win, and I feel there's a strong probability that advertiser use the information to promote certain products. Still, iWon is one of the top ten sites for Internet contesting based on the average daily reach across the Internet and has been repeatedly ranked as a top site on the Internet."

"With so many contests and sweepstakes right at my fingertips my head was spinning," says Carol, "I knew I couldn't possibly enter them all, so I had to pace myself. Even though it can be convenient to enter on the Internet, I wanted to make sure that I allotted enough time for entering contests and sweepstakes the traditional way."

While most traditional contests and sweepstakes are a means to promote a product or service, many on-line contests and sweepstakes, are geared to collecting personal information that can be sold to mass marketers who use the information to target specific demographic groups. Computer technology makes the gathering of on-line information possible, and many so-called contests ask for seemingly irrelevant information.

Carol is not oblivious to these the ulterior motives of online marketers: "Personal information is valuable and is where the company makes most of its money by sharing the information with other companies for a price," she says. "Some examples of the going rates that marketers sell this information for are:

An address: 50 cents
Date of birth: $2.00
Unlisted telephone number: $17.50
Social security number: $8.00
Cell phone number: $10.00
Worker's compensation history: $18.00
Bankruptcy details: $26.50

"Many people don't mind giving out personal information, but I don't like the idea of the world knowing so much about me," she says, "Rather than throw my hat into the very crowded national on-line arena along with millions of other entries, I prefer to enter on-line contests and sweepstakes that are sponsored locally. If I do enter a nationally sponsored contests or sweepstakes I prefer to enter those that are sponsored by familiar well known reputable companies like Coca-cola, Pepsi, Pizza Hut, Frito Lay, Oil of Olay, etc. These companies generally don't ask for a lot of personal information."

As always, when Carol enters a contest or sweepstakes, she enters everyone in her family, and the Internet is no exception. In no time, her relations were all "Winning Big" on the Internet!

"The first thing I won was two tickets to see the Ice Capades. Then I won two tickets to the *Working Woman's Survival Show*, a book called *Entombed*, a Netties Flower Bouquet, a designer's belt and key chain, a Christmas CD, and two tickets to attend a Mannheim Steamroller Concert."

"Everyone in the family was winning something! My daughter Donna won dinner for two at the Outback Restaurant, two tickets to see *Mama Mia*, a $50 Circuit City Gift Card, two tickets to attend a performance of the St. Louis Symphony Orchestra, and a Zatarain's gift box."

"Debbie had a big win on the Internet when she won a trip for four to Jupiter, Florida, to attend the St. Louis Cardinal's Spring Training ... valued at $2,800," says Carol, "She, Donald and their sons David, and Drew had a great time in Florida and got to meet several St. Louis Cardinal baseball players. Other prizes Debbie won are a $75 American Express Gift Card, four tickets to see The (Carlos) Santana Show, $150 Gift Certificate for the Hudson Jewelry Store, two tickets to a Michael Payne Seminar, and two Doctor Phil books."

Carol's strategy for winning on the Internet is to religiously enter everyone in her family every day...even on holidays: "The rules for most contests and sweepstakes on the Internet state one entry per day per e-mail address allowed. For this reason I asked each family member to have individual e-mail addresses...not to share one address."

"For anyone who likes to use a computer, contesting on the Internet can be fun and challenging with so many sites to choose from. Once after I spoke at a contest club meeting one of the club's members told me she had won three cars on the Internet. Now *that* is what I call Winning Big!"

35

"Thanks to the Internet my thread of contesting weaved its way in a different direction," Carol says, "so I decided to write a book about my hobby. Whenever you do something unusual or different, like contesting, people will say, "You should write a book"...so I did."

"I had pretty much mastered the computer, so I decided that now was the time to pursue goal number 11 on my Dream List... WRITE A BOOK.

Carol found a publisher and within the year, her how-to book *Contest Queen* was in print, detailing Carol's success in the contesting world and some of her strategies for winning sweepstakes.

"I got to host book signings at several Borders and Barnes & Nobel Book Stores in the St. Louis area," says Carol, "The managers at the stores treated me like royalty... fresh flowers at my signing table, sodas, snacks, etc. Before I went to the book signings I wanted to come up with something special to write in the books and decided on,
Don't be afraid to follow your dreams and remember, you can create your own luck! I wrote this in every book I signed."

"I asked the manager at the Wal-Mart Store where I worked if Wal-Mart would sell my books. He said it was Wal-Mart's policy not to do business with their employees. I didn't think this was fair and wrote the CEO of the Wal-Mart Corporation and explained that I worked for the company, had written a book, and very much wanted my book to be for sale at Wal-Mart Stores. He agreed and allowed my book to be sold in the St. Louis area Wal-Mart Stores. I hosted book signings at four of the Wal-Mart Stores, including the one were I work."

Carol had met many celebrities because of her contesting, but now she was being treated like a celebrity herself.

"It was great fun!" She says, "People would recognize me at restaurants, in stores, at the mall, at the theater....Ed and I went to the Fox Theater in St. Louis to see a musical and a woman recognized me. She turned to Ed and said,
"You must be Ed. I have the "Contest Queen" book and I read about you." Ed turned a bright pink, but he got a big kick out of all the attention!"

2001 was another traveling year for Carol and Ed. After her prize winnings from *To Tell the Truth* were in the bank; Ed and Carol scheduled a trip to Egypt for the third week in September 2001. In the meanwhile, Carol had won another contest, and the prize was a trip for two to Washington, D.C.! Carol had visited the U.S. capital on a high school trip and was eager to pay it another visit. Together, Ed and Carol explored the houses of government, the historic architecture and the timeless memorials to American heroes and legends.

"We couldn't have visited Washington D.C. at a better time. Though we were there in April, it didn't rain one day during our visit."

"Architecturally, the buildings housing the nation's executive, legislative, and judicial branches of the government are powerful, and after seeing them I feel they help to define us as a people," she says.

"Our trip had been fantastic, but it was time to go home. We had a marvelous time seeing the Nation's capitol... thanks to contesting. At the airport our flight was overbooked. Ed and I agreed to give up our seats and catch a later flight and for doing so received free airline tickets. We decided we'd use the tickets to fly to New York someday."

Shortly after returning home from Washington D.C., Carol received another invitation to attend another time share promotion.

Despite her best attempts to dissuade the salesperson, Ed convinced her to go on the promotion, which promised free tickets to Florida and accommodations at the Epcot Center

"Why not," said Ed, "It's only for three days."

"Once again we listened to a hard sell presentation, and as promised we received airline tickets to Florida," says Carol. "We went the first week in August during my two days off at work that week so I'd only miss one day of work. It was hotter than blazes, but despite the heat we managed to have a good time visiting the various pavilions at the Epcot Center that represent countries from all over the world. It was like seeing the world in a day!"

They especially liked the Chinese Pavilion, prompting Carol to tell Ed they had to visit China someday. He agreed.

Carol and Ed were in the process of packing their suitcases when Donna called, exclaiming,

"Mom, turn on the television! America is being attacked."

Like the rest of the world, Ed and Carol were stupefied and appalled at what they saw, as a newscaster gravely announced the tragic 9-11 attacks.

"We were in shock!" Carol says. "Our children and friends begged us not to go to Egypt, so we cancelled our trip and were fortunate that our travel agent gave us travel vouchers for a future trip. Many travelers weren't as lucky and lost the money they had paid for trips. I had vacation time approved at work and wanted to go somewhere, but the airlines weren't flying. Ed and I decided we'd take a Greyhound bus and go and see Mt. Rushmore in South Dakota."

36

"Even though the trip to Mount Rushmore National Memorial was an impromptu trip, it turned out to be a great trip!" Carol remembers, "What we liked about traveling on a Greyhound bus was that the bus didn't travel on interstate highways, but instead traveled mostly on two lane highways. This transcended an ordinary traveling experience into a sightseeing adventure. We found that going by bus is a great way to see America!"

The tour bus snaked its way through the Midwest, and Carol experienced Mt. Rushmore in all its glory, along with other heritage sites of the region, such as the battlefields of the 19th century Indian Wars, and the Crazy Horse Memorial.

"I didn't use all my vacation time from work for the trip to Mount Rushmore, so I still had a few days left for another trip," says Carol, "We were still apprehensive about flying because of 9-11, so we decided it might be fun to take a train trip.

After some deliberation, Carol and Ed decided they'd like to spend new Year's Eve in San Antonio, Texas. They boarded an Amtrak train bound for San Antonio, although she'd visited the city in the past as well.

"I had been to San Antonio with Don after I'd won a trip to this unique city," Carol explains, "but we went in the summer and the River walk wasn't decorated. I thought it would great to go there during the holidays. Ed had never been to San Antonio and very much wanted to see the Alamo."

As a bonus, Carol had started to receive royalty checks from the sale of her book, *Contest Queen*, and found this money a great boon for her continual traveling.

After a lengthily cross-country train ride, Carol and Ed arrived in the dead of night in San Antonio.

The following morning, after visiting the ruins of the Alamo, the duo indulged in some shopping in downtown San Antonio. "I've never known a man who likes to shop as much as Ed!" Carol says.

Spending New Years Eve in San Antonio was great fun. They boarded a riverboat at the lagoon for a romantic ride down the Rio Grande: "As Ed and I ensconced ourselves in the back of the boat I felt like I was back in Venice, Italy... riding in a gondola boat. I told Ed,
"Wouldn't it be great if St. Louis had a river running through downtown like this?"
He said,
"You know, the River Des Peres could be transformed into an attraction like this."

During the years that Ed and Carol were busy traveling, the rest of her family was busy reaping the fruits of their matriarch's contesting endeavors. "I would bring sweepstakes blanks with me on trips to fill out on the airplane, the bus, the train ...I'd work on the blanks during the evenings in our hotel room," Carol says, "After we'd return home I would mail the entry blanks or drop them off at the store that was sponsoring the sweepstakes. I had to be sure that we'd be back from the trip before the expiration date of the sweepstakes."

Because of Carol's dedication in staying on top of sweepstakes, her extended family has been showered with winnings. Scores of sporting and concert tickets, clothing, gift certificates, electronics, collectable memorabilia, and exotic services were heaped upon them during Carol's absences.

In early 2002, Carol and Ed received the travel vouchers from their aborted voyage to Egypt and prepared to embark on another adventure around the world. They already had a destination in mind:

China.

37

Carol's visit to China was a momentous event in her life, and she describes it as "my favorite place I've ever been to." Just being able to visit the Communist state was a marvel to her itself: When she'd been born, China was divided into multiple, competing warlord states. For decades after, it had been a hostile, secretive dictatorship. Now, the regime was open to the outside world, a modernized, bustling power on the rise...all within Carol's lifetime.

"China is a beautiful country with stunning landscapes and the people are the most gregarious and friendliest people I've ever met," she says, "They like to laugh and have a great sense of humor, yet they are most gracious. Wherever we went we were offered green tea, which I love and still drink today."

Despite the positive impression of China she gained from her visit, Carol was not oblivious to the dark side of the regime, which poked its head through the happy, tourist-friendly façade: "I brought several key chains with a U.S. penny in them with me to give to Chinese people that I might meet. One day I tried to give a key chain to a cute little girl, but her grandmother forbade the girl to take it. I later learned that Chinese people are not allowed to accept gifts from foreigners, or to invite foreigners into their homes."

After a seventeen hour flight from St. Louis, Carol and Ed touched ground in Beijing, where they were met a tour guide named Wang, who proceeded to show the travelers around one of the most populated cities in the world. They toured the Forbidden City, the Temple of Heaven, structures from the bygone age of the Chinese emperors. They stood in Tiananmen Square, where China's hopes for reform and democracy were cruelly snuffed out a decade before. Carol was in awe of the place.

"As we stood admiring the buildings, a young girl approached Wang and asked if Ed would be willing to have his picture taken with her mother," remembers Carol, "Laughing, Ed agreed and posed with a shy little giggling woman who stood next to Ed while their picture was taken. After they left Wang told Ed the girl and her mother thought he was a "General". Ed does look like a general since he's so tall and sports a flat top hair cut."

The next day, Carol and Ed went to see the Great Wall of China, a necessity for Carol who wanted to check off goal number 13 on her Dream List... "CLIMB THE GREAT WALL OF CHINA."

"We could barely manage to climb the wall to the first tower and our legs hurt for two days afterward," recounts Carol, "It was difficult for us to climb because some of the steps are higher than others and we couldn't get a rhythm going up or coming down the steps. Still it was a thrill to have had the opportunity to climb the Great Wall of China and I couldn't wait to tell my grandchildren about it."

The tour guide, Wang, was informative and knowledgeable about his countries history, but Carol noticed over time that he seemed to be a mouthpiece for the policies of his government. On the return from the Great Wall, the tour bus took a route through a slum of Beijing, riddled with unsavory characters.

"Wang told us that we were perfectly safe because China is a Communist country and there's very little crime," says Carol, "He said criminals are punished harshly."

The travelers still had some free time in Beijing before going on to the next city, and decided to use it to carry out their usual errands: collecting souvenirs and acquiring fire patches for Donald back home. Along the way, they saw aspects of Beijing that Wang would probably rather they hadn't.

"We got lost trying to find the firehouse and went into a hospital instead," says Carol, "We were shocked at how dismal and out of date the hospital was. We saw that the fire station was across the street from the hospital, and tried to cross the street but were almost run down by hundreds of fast moving bicyclist."

"We eventually made it across the street to the fire station, but none of the firefighters spoke English," she says, "I showed them a photo of Donald in his uniform that was in my billfold and the fire patches that I had brought with me, so they could understood my mission. They gave me several medals and epaulets for his collection, but no patches. Wang later told me that Chinese firefighters don't wear patches on their uniforms because firemen in China also serve as policemen."

In the city of Xi'an, Carol and Ed endured another case of culture shock which reminded them that China is, unfortunately, riddled with corruption: "Our van was stopped by the police. The policeman said the van driver had passed a military vehicle, but none of us in the van saw a military vehicle," says Carol, "The guide said that in China you pay your fine directly to the policeman who stops you, and if you argue your fine is increased."

Though the tour company as a matter of course reimburses its customers who are extorted in this mAnnr, this blatant case of bribery and corruption would stick out in Carol's mind for a long time to come, reminding her that she was but a stranger in a strange land. There were other unsettling issues raised, as well…even from the tour guides themselves.

"(Our guide) told us that her younger brother had died from malnutrition because her parents couldn't afford to buy milk," says Carol, "She said that even today the people in China will greet each other not with, "Good morning, how are you?" but with "Have you eaten today?" This is a fall back to when the people in China were starving."

Some time later, the tour group made its way to Shanghai, China's largest city, where Carol observed the contrast in the city between old world charm and the modern skyline. Because there are no labor unions in China, the city is in a constant state of construction and modernization. Everywhere Carol went, she saw the city getting ready for the 2008 Olympic Games…building stadiums and hotels, repairing roads and updating public infrastructure. "My favorite place in Shanghai is Old Shanghai," she says, "I loved strolling through the 400 year old Yuyuan

Winning Big

Gardens where China's oldest, most famous tea house is located. A wall with a giant dragon on top surrounds the beautiful garden. (The district) exemplifies China's old charm and the shopping is good. I purchased key chains and writing pens for my fellow associates at Wal-Mart. China has unique, unusual souvenirs and it was fun to barter (with the merchants)."

The last city on our tour was Hong Kong, for many years a British protectorate. Hong Kong is a "Special Administrative Region" of China, and its prosperous capitalist economy is untouched by the state. British influences are apparent throughout the city. At the conclusion of their tour, Carol and Ed had two days to do what they wished in China.

"This was the perfect opportunity for me to visit a Wal-Mart Store," says Carol, "I'd gotten the addresses of Wal-Mart Stores in China from the personal department at my store, The nearest Wal-Mart to Hong Kong was in Shenzhen, China and to get there we'd have to take a train back to Mainland China. I don't think many men would have agreed, but Ed, bless his heart, said he'd come with me."

Though Carol and Ed wouldn't have the benefit of a tour guide, Carol devised a solution: "Before we left the hotel I asked a clerk at the desk to write a few notes for us in Chinese that we could use to get around. I had her write in Chinese, "Where is the toilet?" Then I'd write the message under her Chinese writings in English. Other questions I asked her to write were, "Can you direct me to the train station?", "Where can I catch a taxi?", "Can you take us to the Wal-Mart Store?" It worked! All we had to do was hold up a specific question and we were able to get help and directions."

It was a long train ride back to the Mainland, and once they there, Carol and Ed had to buy a one-day visa and clear customs, and then look for a taxi to take them to the Wal-Mart Store.

"It wasn't long before we arrived at Shenzhen Wal-Mart Super Center," says Carol, "We were surprised at the size of the Super Center...it was one city block long and three stories tall."

"A Customer Service Manager approached us as we entered, and much to our delight, he spoke English. He was very friendly and offered to serve as an interpreter," she says, "What a Godsend he was, introducing us to the General Manager of the store, her assistants, and other workers at the store. He told them that I worked for a Wal-Mart Store in the United States and had brought gifts from my store in Illinois. The manager was thrilled and she gave me a score of Chinese Wal-Mart souvenirs. As she gave us a tour of the store, many of the Associates bowed to us. We got some great photos of the Chinese Wal-Mart for our store back home."

"On our last day in Hong Kong, I walked to a Hong Kong Fire Department to exchange fire patches," Carol says, "The Hong Kong firefighters spoke the best English of all the people I encountered in China, except for our tour guides and the clerks at the hotels. The firemen told me they had learned to speak English while training for the fire service in New York City."

The firemen were happy to trade patches and gave Carol a tour of their modern facility before she made her way back to the hotel and noticed contests offering everything from new cars to the chance to meet Canadian actress Pamela Anderson.

All too soon, the trip to China was over and it was time to pack for the journey home. Everywhere she went, Carol was amazed by the differences between East and West: "In all the cities we visited I only saw three dogs, two cats, no pigeons, and very few birds. I saw very few people with a weight problem. Most of the businesses were overstaffed and it was not unusual to have three or four waitresses serve us in a restaurant. There were policemen on every street corner," she says. "The toilets in China are most unusual. I asked a Chinese woman why they have holes in the floors for toilets? She said, 'We don't sit on a seat like you do on Western toilets, but choose to squat over an opening in the floor because we feel this is more sanitary. To use an Eastern toilet not one part of the body touches the fixture."

After arriving home, Carol went back to work and gave the Wal-Mart gifts from China to her store. Many of the items she'd purchased were raffled off to raise money for the Children's Miracle Network. Carol looks back on her voyage to China as a huge learning experience and a highlight of her world travels.

"They say China is a sleeping giant," she says, "But from what I saw, I'd say the giant is waking up!"

38

"One of the first things I did after we returned home from China was to write an article about our trip for the Suburban Journals Newspaper," says Carol, "and it was a hit with the readers. The success with that article prompted me to submit another article about the Chinese Wal-Mart store for a newspaper produced by and for associates of Wal-Mart. I received a lot of positive feedback from fellow associates and a letter from Tom Underwood, Vice President for Wal-Mart, telling me how much he enjoyed reading the article and how happy he was that I'd had such a good experience visiting the Chinese Wal-Mart."

As spring turned into summer, Ed and Carol knew they had to make a decision as to where they wanted to travel using the free airline vouchers we had received for giving up their seats on the return trip from Washington D.C. After much thought, they decided to book a twelve day bus trip through the New England states. Carol relates some highlights of her trip through the region:

"We flew for free to New York City where we stayed overnight before boarding a bus for our Fall Foliage Tour. It was a beautiful sunny fall day as our bus departed from Manhattan and followed the Connecticut shore via New Haven, where Yale University is located. We visited Boston, and saw numerous landmarks that reflect the importance that this New England city played in early American history. We had enough time here to walk to a fire station and exchange fire patches for Donald's collection."

"As we continued on our journey we saw many lighthouses along the way. At Portland, Maine we visited the Portland Headlight Lighthouse...the oldest lighthouse in Maine. We drove through Augusta, Maine's capital, before coming to the popular seaside resort of Bar Harbor. The resort town is situated on Mount Desert Island, one of the most beautiful islands in the Atlantic and site of Acadia National Park, a major wildlife sanctuary. We saw the Dolly Parton Mountain Peaks and Cadillac Mountain, highest point on the Atlantic coast. During the drive we saw some of New

England's most spectacular scenery and I told Ed, "This looks like one of God's paintings."

"The drive was especially scenic along the Hudson River Valley to Albany, New York's state capital. The leavews were ablaze with colour. We arrived late in the afternoon at the New York Helmsley Hotel in Manhattan, where we would be staying the last two days of our trip."

"The following morning we were treated to a tour of New York City's most popular sights: Times Square, Greenwich Village, St. Patrick's Cathedral, the Empire State Building, Wall Street, and Chinatown. The second day was a free day to do as we wished before packing for our return trip home. Ed and I decided to take a double-decker bus to Battery Park and catch a ferry boat to Ellis Island and the Statue of Liberty. As we sat on the top deck of the bus, the wind made my hair stand straight up but I didn't care because we were going home the next day. At Battery Park we saw a temporary memorial to the 9-11 tragedy...the Twin Tower Plaza Globe and Flames that was found in the rubble of the buildings. I took Ed's picture standing in front of the memorial."

"After the visit to Ellis Island we decided to go to Ground Zero, the site where the Twin Towers had stood before the 9-11 terrorist attack. I was surprised at my gut wrenching emotions as we walked to the edge of a giant hole in the ground and starred in stupefaction through fencing that had been installed at the site. I remembered having watched the tragedy on television and couldn't believe I was actually at the place it had happened. As I thought of all the innocent people who had died on that horrific day it felt as though a giant had put his fist in my solar plexus. Ed said something sotto voce, his voice strident and angry that I couldn't understand. We stayed at "Ground Zero" much longer than we had anticipated because it was difficult to pull ourselves away."

At the end of it all, it was time to return home, once again.

"Generally on a return flight from one of our trips Ed and don't talk much about the trip we have just been on. Instead we will talk about where we want to go next," Carol says, "We agreed that 2002 had been a wonderful traveling year then we discussed where we wanted to go in 2003. Egypt is always foremost on our agenda, but we are reluctant to travel to this unstable part of the world."

39

After Carol returned home her latest excursion, people started coming into Wal-Mart to tell me what prizes they'd won using her techniques for "Winning Big."

"One man told me he had won an expensive camera in a drawing, by crumbling up his entry before dropping it into a box" says Carol. "A lady told me she had won a trip to Las Vegas by drawing a roulette wheel on her mail-in entry, and another customer told me he'd won a prize on the Internet by entering a sweepstakes once every day at a local radio station site. They were all thrilled, and I told them I knew how they felt and that I was happy for them...but warned them that contesting can become addictive."

After Christmas had passed, Ed and Carol found that they'd acquired enough frequent flier miles in their accounts to cover the cost of a trip to England, and quickly arranged a comprehensive tour of the British Isles. In the meantime, they would undertake a pilgrimage that all Americans must experience at one time or another: Carol and Ed were going to Graceland.

They traveled by Amtrak to Memphis, Tennessee, to see the home of Elvis Presley.

"Most kings live in castles, but Elvis had a home," says Carol, "We entered a world that is exactly as it was in the 1970s. The house tour offered a unique glimpse into the personal life of Elvis and we were able to experience some of the magic of his life."

Carol and Ed toured Graceland and then explored the Memphis region, experiencing the rich cultural heritage of the South. As they made their way home from another journey, Ed plAnnd to make his next move.

"Soon after we returned from Memphis, Ed proposed marriage

again," says Carol, "It seemed he held my eyes for an interminable time before he showed me a ring he had purchased. He said we could honeymoon in Egypt, but I told him I didn't want to get married because I was afraid that if we married it would jeopardize our relationship... I was afraid to take the plunge after my 38-year marriage had ended."

"When Ed came along, he gave my life new meaning by bringing fun and adventure into my existence. When I was with him I was eager for what each new day might bring. Ed was a wonderful companion...enthusiastic, jovial, and interested in everything I did. He brought my life full circle...I felt truly alive again. I was afraid if we got married it would ruin the happiness we had found together. Ed accepted the fact that I didn't want to get married and he never asked me again."

40

"One of the most satisfying things about contesting," Carol says, "is that it affords me the opportunity to help my family and friends. My hobby has positively enriched the lives of my entire family and that makes me happy. Everyone in my family has been able to take trips and enjoy owning various material things they may never have bought for themselves."

When Carol ends up with duplicate prizes or something she doesn't need, she passes it along to the community to share her good luck: "I once won four duplicate TV sets. I gave one television to a man whose television was broken and he didn't have the funds to get it repaired or to buy a new one. I gave another television to my sister and her husband after their set was stolen. I offered another television to a teen center to use as a raffle prize."

Another way that Carol has been able to help family and friends is by giving advice from the interview course she took in college about how to "Win Big" and get the important job they are seeking. "At Wal-Mart there are a lot of teenagers and college students who have, or will soon be going out into the workplace," says Carol, "Through the years I have tried to help them and the children of my friends. Occasionally one of them will come into the store or call me to thank me for having helped them land their dream job."

"One young man who worked at Wal-Mart wanted to get employment at the Chrysler Plant in Fenton, Missouri. I gave him a copy of my "interviewing" notes and during our lunchtime we would role-play his interview. He was thrilled when he got the job!"

Shortly before Carol left for the British Isles, she won two tickets to see a Broadway play in St. Louis. As she was opening a frozen bottle of water from her purse during the intermission, she accidentally drenched the man in the seat beside her. Though the man was soaked, "he handled it graciously," Carol says.

"He said his wife was a contesting enthusiast and she had won their tickets as well. I told them about my book and his wife said she would certainly be ordering one."

Carol and Ed traveled to the British Isles in 2003, arriving in London in the midst of the heat wave that held Europe in its molten grip all summer. Their trip couldn't have come at a more hazardous time because the heat in Europe that summer would eventually kill some 35,000 people!

"Hundreds of people had already died because of the heat. Our hotel didn't have air-conditioning...it normally doesn't get that warm in London...the heat was unbearable. Our hotel window only opened out a few inches, so it was suffocating in our room with the temperature well over 100 degrees," Carol says.

Though they were not felled by the heat, it hampered their sleep and during their stay in London, they were un-rested and weary. In addition, their tours of London took them back to attractions they had already explored. They were glad when the time came to leave the sweltering city, and found the countryside to be much cooler.

"Our first stops upon leaving London were Hampton Court Palace; Runnymede where King John sealed the Magna Carta; Oxford University where Britain's elite receive an outstanding education and where former President Clinton attended school; and Blaydon where Sir Winston Churchill lies buried within sight of his birthplace, Blenheim Palace ... the only non-royal palace in Britain," recounts Carol.

The tour visited Stratford-upon-Avon, birthplace of William Shakespeare, before stopping in Coventry for the night. The next morning, the tour passed Sherwood Forest, the traditional setting of the Robin Hood tales, and engaged in a walking tour of York, Britain's most authentic medieval city.

"We were excited the next day to be going to Scotland. On the way we stopped at Hadrian's Wall, a Roman coast-to-coast wall built as a defense against marauding northern tribes. It was no Great Wall of China, but it was interesting," Carol says. The tour continued north, crossing the Scottish border before stopping for the night in Edinburgh.

In Scotland, they toured ancient castles and visited relics of a bygone age.

"Our second day in Edinburgh was scheduled for the famous "Tattoo." Anyone wishing to attend the Tattoo had to pay $100 at the time they booked the tour because tickets are hard to come by and sell out way before the event," Carol explains, "Ed and I had opted not to sign up since we didn't really know what it was. We learned this Tattoo would be Scotland's 54th celebration of music, dance, and spectacle set against the impressive backdrop of Edinburgh Castle. We wished we had signed up for the tattoo, but since we didn't we had to fill our day with something else to do while the others on the tour went to the Tattoo."

"We spent part of the day exploring the quaint streets of the city and were surprised to see a statue of Abraham Lincoln in Scotland. We learned the statue was there because Scots fought in the U.S. Civil War. At the Edinburgh firehouse I met the first and only woman firefighter I've met while visiting fire stations all over the world. She gave me a thick wool sweater that the Scottish firefighters wear during the cold winters to take home to Donald."

Departing Edinburgh and rolling south, the tour made stops in Liverpool and Lockerbie, site of the infamous Pan-America bombing.

"At Liverpool we were booked in the Britannia Adelphi Hotel, the same hotel that the passengers of the Titanic stayed before their fateful cruise," Carol recalls, "A visit to The Cavern pub where the Beatles first performed was not on the itinerary of the tour, but Ed and I wanted to see it, so we went there on our own and when we got there we saw a statue of John Lennon over the entrance of the pub."

"The next day we crossed the border from Scotland into North Wales. Our bus followed the coast and stopped at the town,

Llanfairpwllgwyngyll. The guide offered a free trip to anyone who could pronounce the name of the town. Nobody on the tour even tried, and this was one contest I wasn't about to attempt!"

"At Holyhead, we boarded a Ferry across the Irish Sea crossing to the city of Dublin, capital of the Republic of Ireland. We enjoyed a city tour through Eire's capital that included a stop at St. Patrick's Cathedral where St. Patrick is said to have baptized his first Christian. The guide said the Euro is used in Ireland and that food, goods, and petrol are expensive. Hats are so expensive that people rent them from a hat service!"

Before they'd left home, Ed and Carol made arrangements to spend a night at an authentic Irish castle, the Clontarf Castle, which is over nine hundred years old. This would fulfill another goal on Carol's Dream List...TO SLEEP IN A CASTLE.

"The tour bus took us to the castle, but we were told that we'd have to catch a taxi in the morning to the hotel where the tour group would be staying. As we entered the castle I felt like we'd just been transmuted into a world of kings, queens, and knights. The castle looked much like I imagined an old castle would look. It has a rugged interior with timbers that are visible. The floors are done in rock and I couldn't help but think of all the kings and queens who had treaded these floors as they danced and dined."

"We motored through County Cork to Blarney...famous for its magical Stone of Eloquence in the Blarney Castle. Tradition dictates that the stone has the power of conferring eloquence on all who kiss it. To kiss the Blarney Stone was another goal on my Dream List, and we had to go in single file up a torrent in the Blarney Castle to a 3rd floor. It was a difficult climb and I felt claustrophobic. When we got to the stone which is set in a wall below some battlements, we had to hang out a window to kiss it while an old man held us by our legs so we wouldn't fall out the window. I told Ed this will make an interesting story to tell the grandchildren."

"It didn't take long the next day to cross St. George's Channel to South Wales. We stopped at Cardiff, Wales' capital city, where we saw Cardiff Castle. We crossed the spectacular Seven

Bridges back into England and drove past Cornwall, England (King Arthur's territory), past Canterbury, (land of Camelot), and Glassenburgh, where King Arthur and Genevieve are said to be buried."

When the tour entered the old Roman city of Bath, the ancient relics made Ed feel like he was back in Italy, not England! "The Roman baths, Temples of Sulis Minerva are among the finest Roman remains in Britain," says Carol, "At their heart is Britain's only hot springs, where the Celtic and Classical worlds meet in a magnificent complex of stone used for worship, cleansing, and healing. Queen Victoria, Jane Austin, and Charles Dickens liked to go to Bath."

From Bath, Carol and Ed went to prehistoric Stonehenge, one of the most visited places in England. How the enigmatic structure was constructed remains a mystery, with the giant boulders being impossible to move with ancient technology.

"As always our trip was over too soon, a waking dream, but I had a ton of photos for my travel scrapbooks. It had been a wonderful trip with something interesting around every bend!"

41

In the summer of 2004, Ed won a trip to the Olympics in Athens, Greece...crediting them with even more frequent flier miles: "Thanks to the frequent flier miles we accumulated from the trip to Athens, and other vacations, we had accrued enough miles for another trip," says Carol. "All we had to do was decide where we wanted to go."

"Ed said he had always wanted to see Hawaii and asked how I felt about going on a Hawaiian cruise. I told him I'd been to Hawaii four times, but would go on a Hawaiian cruise if we could book a cruise that also went through the South Pacific so I could check off Goal number 19 on my Dream List... CRUISE THE SOUTH PACIFIC. Ed agreed and we booked a cruise for October 2004."

Carol and Ed spent a few days touring the sights of the Hawaiian island of Oahu, and according to Carol, Ed was captivated by the locale: "Ed said he couldn't get over how beautiful Hawaii is. I told him there would be more beauty to see as we visited the other Hawaiian Islands." After a few days in the Islands, they journeyed aboard the cruise linger *Norwegian Wind* to begin their cruise of the south Pacific.

One of the first stops the cruise liner made was at Fanning Island, in the tiny south Pacific Republic of Kiribati. "A visit to remote Fanning Island is a once in a life-time experience and was the highlight of the trip for me," says Carol, "Fanning Island is located a thousand miles south of Hawaii. There's no electricity, telephones, cars, or a functioning airport on the lush island which serves as a private getaway and weekly port of call for Norwegian Cruise Lines. Prior to that, the only ships that visited here were Australian supply ships that arrived 2-3 times per year – the islanders' only link to the modern world."

There is only one harbor on the island, English Harbor, which is situated within a barrier reef near the southwestern part of the island. Passengers on the cruise ship had to be tendered to the island by small boats because the water around the island is too shallow to accommodate a big ship. The island is home to a small post office where it's possible to mail a letter or postcard. Delivery, however, can take up to 3 months. Because of Fanning Island's seclusion, a Republic of Kiribati stamp is very much prized by philatelists.

"It was interesting to find islanders don't understand the concept of ownership," says Carol, "If one of the natives rides a bicycle to a neighboring village and leaves it, another islander can take the bike. Two cruise line employees live on the island and it is their job to get the island ready for weekly visitors from the cruise ships. NCL has provided them with a generator so they can watch video movies. Some islanders found the VHS tapes, and being ignorant of their purpose made "grass skirts" from the film."

"Our visit to remote Fanning Island was a magical fun-filled day in paradise that Ed and I treasure and will never forget. I must say, of all the places I have traveled in the world this was one place I didn't see any contests or sweepstakes!"

After a few more days at sea, the ship made a return to Hawaii and visited a small whaling village on the outskirts of the islands. Carol saw this as a perfect opportunity to cross another item off her Dream List: "I suggested to Ed that we go on a whale watch and he thought that was a great idea...we got to see several huge whales up-close and personal as a guide on the boat interpreted their behavior. I was able to check off goal number 8 on my Dream List ... "SEE A WHALE IN ITS NATURAL HABITAT.""

Another stop the cruise made was on the Hawaiian island of Kona, home to one of Wal-Marts more far-flung locations. "Ed and I wanted to visit a Wal-Mart Store in Hawaii and we found the store in Kona to be the most beautiful Wal-Mart Store we've ever visited," she reports, "Located along the side of a mountain above the Pacific Ocean, the view was spectacular. From the front of the store we could see our cruise ship anchored in the ocean. I talked with a greeter at the store and she told me she was originally from South Dakota and that she and her husband had retired in Hawaii."

Soon after arriving back in Honolulu, it was time to return to the American mainland. "Ed said he was sad to be leaving such a beautiful place and hoped we'd return someday. I told him, "Who knows what the future holds? Perhaps we will return someday.""

42

In the spring of 2005, Carol got another call from the local casting agency that still had her name on file. They were looking for extras to appear in the film *The Beauty and Apocalypse.*, being filmed in Waterloo, Illinois.

"The scene that I was in was filmed at night at a junkyard. It was a cold night and spooky at the junkyard," she says, "A film crew brought a Winnebago to the site to be used as a dressing room for the actors and extras. A big delivery truck that was loaded with costumes was parked next to the Winnebago. The first place I had to go after I arrived at the junkyard was to the truck where I was fitted with a pair of ripped jeans, old shoes, and a long tattered green coat. I put the clothing on in the back of the Winnebago and then a make-up artist made me look dirty and she tousled my hair until it looked like I hadn't combed my hair in a week."

"The scene I was in was a funeral for the "Beauty." She was in a make shift casket with brightly lit pole torches stuck in the ground at each end of the casket. I was one of the mourners at the funeral and had to stand in front of the casket and look very sad. It was a windy night and some hot embers from the torches blew into the casket. She quickly sat up and cursed, "Keep that…fire off me! The whole scene was surreal, and it was a most interesting night!"

2005 was another year of fruitful travel for Carol and her family, as she took a Mediterranean cruise with her daughter Donna, and grandchildren Amanda & Jimmy.

"Donna and I hoped the trip would instill a love of travel for Amanda and Jimmy. It's one thing to read about all the exciting places in the world, but another thing to actually go there, because travel enhances your life so much," Carol points out.

They visited ports along the European coast; some of them

Winning Big

places Carol and Ed had visited on their trip through Europe, some of them new, including Barcelona, Sicily, and Dubrovnik, Croatia.

After Carol returned home from the Mediterranean, she noticed there was only one goal left on her Dream List... number fifteen, "TO SEE THE WORLD": "I felt I had seen much of the world and could in good conscience check this off the list," she says, "After I did that, it didn't feel right not to have a list of goals to try to achieve since I had been doing it for so long. I decided to compile another Dream List. Ed rolled his eyes in disbelief, thinking that since I had achieved all my goals I would be done with it. Though I was older, my passion for life hadn't dimmed and I found that having dreams helped me to stay young."

After much thought, Carol compiled the following list:

1. Be a guest on Oprah's show.
2. See the Sequoia trees.
3. Swim with the Dolphins.
4. Visit Egypt and see the Pyramids and ride a camel.
5. Take a hot air balloon ride.
6. Visit Transylvania in Romania and see Dracula's Castle.
7. Write another book (Fiction).
8. Find a way to take all my family on a cruise.
9. Be a contestant in the Pillsbury bake-off contest.
10. Spend a day at a luxurious spa.
11. Land a walk-on part for a soap opera.
12. Ride the Bullet Train in Japan.
13. Meet Dr. Phil.
14. Find more ways to support the Children's Miracle Network charity.
15. Take a train trip across Canada.
16. Go white water rafting.
17. Find a way to open a safe house for battered women in my town.
18. Dig for diamonds in Arkansas
19. Help my granddaughter realize her dream of opening an animal sanctuary.
20. See my life story made into a movie.

Unlike her first Dream List, designed to take Carol around the world and to do things many never get a chance to do, this new list contained goals to help her live life to the fullest and also to give back to the world, to leave it a better place than she found it. Carol explains why this is so:

> "One day while I was at work a fellow associate showed me a National Examiner tabloid offering its readers a chance to win $50 for an article about "The Day That Changed My Life."
>
> "You like to write, you ought to submit an article," my friend insisted.
>
> "I thought it would be challenging to write an article for a national publication, but I had no idea what to write about. Then I remembered my fortieth birthday and how I had made a Dream List of goals I wanted to accomplish. I decided to write about how this had changed my life. I wrote how I'd read that when Benjamin Franklin was in his thirties, he was having trouble getting his life together until he hit on the strategy of writing down what he wanted out of life. He referred to his list frequently and was eventually able to make great advances and increased his contributions to America life. I wrote how I had felt time passing and didn't want to wake up at age sixty-five and regret all the things I had never done, so I took stock of my life and created a list of twenty dreams that I wanted to make come true. I placed the list on my refrigerator door determined to make every single wish on the list come true. It took some time to accomplish my goals, and I wrote how my contesting had helped me to accomplish many of them. I concluded my article by telling them how my journey had taught me to live a richer, more meaningful life full of passion and adventure."

A reporter from the tabloid contacted Carol a few weeks after to tell her she'd won: "When the article was published there were photos of me with Oprah, of Ed and I standing on The Great Wall Of China, of me in my depression era costume working as an extra in the movie *King of the Hill*, and last, but not least, my favourite photo: me receiving my diploma as I graduated from college."

This appearance heralded a tidal wave of recognition for Carol's life achievements, with newspapers and magazines falling over each other to interview Carol and bring her inspirational story to the masses.

"Soon after, I received another call...this time a reporter from the popular national women's magazine, *Woman's World*, asking if I would do an interview for the magazine. My head was spinning from all the attention, but I agreed to do the interview," she says, "The writer mentioned how I didn't want to look back on my life and regret missing out on things, so I'd made a list of my dreams and then set out to make each and every one of them come true."

These articles validated Carol's own self-taught techniques for living a fulfilling and successful life with commentary from noted life-coaches and self-improvement guru's, all of whom agreed with the method of writing down long-term goals to strive for. Carol also found validation of her methods in a number of books written by her contemporaries:

"Mary Allen, a nationally known and accredited life-coach and author of *The Power of Inner Choice: 12 Steps to Living a Life You Love*, wrote,

"You have to believe you deserve the things you want. Then, you have to act to make your dreams come true."

After a while, Carol thought she was done with interviews for the news media, but no sooner had she come to that conclusion did a local PBS affiliate contact her to tape a segment for public television. Carol has come to consider this the best TV interview she's ever done. The interview was a great success and was aired many times on PBS. (Authors note: The segment can be viewed online thanks to Youtube by typing in the keywords 'Carol Shaffer'.)

Shortly thereafter, Carol and Ed embarked on a trans-Canadian rail trip to see more of their neighbour to the north. The trip began in Toronto, where Carol had lived back in the 1960s. Carol found that the once-familiar skyline had changed strikingly in four decades, but marvelled at the cosmopolitan diversity and grandeur of Toronto, which she describes as "a Mecca of film, fashion and publishing." After taking in the sights of Ontario's provincial capital, Carol and Ed made their way to Union Station and got onboard a luxurious cross-country rail car for the rest of their trip.

"As we traveled across the vast plains of Ontario,

Saskatchewan, and Manitoba provinces there was plenty of time to gaze out the window and savour the sweeping views of a landscape immersed in emerald green spruce and white birch trees," she says.

"This first leg of our journey ended at the Rocky Mountain town of Jasper, Alberta. It was here that we got our first up close look at the stunningly beautiful Canadian Rockies." Upon arrival, they proceeded to tour the beautiful Jasper and Banff national parks, including a walk on the famous Athabasca glacier, a giant ice cube as deep as Toronto's CN Tower is high.

"There is an innate presence of nature in the Rockies, a natural richness that is becoming increasingly rare today, so it is no wonder so many people want to go there," observes Carol.

"Our trans-Canadian train adventure ended in Vancouver where we had two days to explore the beautiful city before flying home," she says, "There is much to see and do in Vancouver, as well as the surrounding areas…north of Vancouver is the town of Whistler which will be hosting the 2010 Winter Olympics. The Trans-Canadian Train Adventure was a great adventure that Ed and I highly recommended to our friends after we got back home."

And as a bonus, Carol got to check off goal number fifteen on her new dream list!

43

In 2006, Carol found numerous ways to fill her schedule. She found a way to fuse her innate creative nature with her passion fort travel by decorating each room in her condo with the décor of nations she'd visited in her travels with Ed. This way, their journeys would forever be in the front of their minds, and the memories they had forged would never fade. Still, there was more traveling to be done: "Ed and I didn't have any travel plans for 2006. I suggested we go to California and see the big Sequoia trees," Carol says, "and it let me check off goal number two on my new dream list...SEE THE SEQUOIA TREES."

The year 2007 arrived and with it came new opportunities for contesting to come into Carol's life. She enjoyed another string of victories, rewarding her with free tickets to sports games and cultural events in St. Louis.

"As I do every year, I entered the Publishers Clearing House Sweepstakes," Carol says, "This time, however, I entered the sweepstakes on-line. People often tell me they don't enter the Publishers Clearing House Sweepstakes because they assume they have to place an order to win. I tell them not to be fooled by the sweepstakes promoter's rhetoric. Just as there are rules for contestants to follow in order to enter a sweepstakes, there are also rules that the sponsors of sweepstakes must adhere to... such as not requiring contestants to order a product, or to pay a fee in order to enter and win a sweepstakes."

The Deceptive Mail Prevention and Enforcement Act went into effect on April 12, 2000. The Act grants greater authority to the U.S. Postal Service to protect the public against deceptive mailings and to help ensure that everyone who enters a sweepstakes has an equal chance of winning whether they place an order or not. The law applies only to sweepstakes sent through the U.S. Mail, not to sweepstakes conducted on the Internet or telephone, unless the mail is used. This law prohibits certain false representations in sweepstakes promotions such as:

1) Telling a person that he/she is a winner, unless they have actually won.

2) Stating that a person must order something in order to win, or that a person must send proof of a previous purchase, or be required to make or purchase or that person may not receive future sweepstakes mailings.

3) Including a fake check in the sweepstakes solicitation, unless it is clearly stated that the check has no cash value.

4) Using a seal, name, or term that might give the impression that the sweepstakes is somehow connected to the federal government.

The Act requires that all disclosures must be clearly and conspicuously displayed and readily visible. The Act gives the contestants the right to stop receiving sweepstakes mailings....the sweepstakes sponsors are required to provide a reasonable way to request that a name be removed from their list. (If an individual makes a request in writing that their name be removed, the sponsor must refrain from sending an entry to that person for five years. If the sponsor fails to remove a name, the person receiving the sweepstakes can sue in a small claims court.

"Sometimes people ask why the sponsor of a sweepstakes provides separate "yes" and "no" envelopes for entries. These envelopes are used to help those people who wish to order a product to receive their order faster," explains Carol, "Thanks to the Deceptive Mail Prevention and Enforcement Act people sending a "no" response envelope have an equal chance of winning."

On June 26, 2001, Publishers Clearing House agreed to a $34 million settlement in 26 states. The sponsor attracted the attention of state authorities because so many people complained that the mailings made them believe they would have a better chance of winning if they ordered magazines from the company. The authorities alleged that Publisher Clearing House used other deceptive practices in its sweepstakes mailings such as including the phrase "You are a Winner!" on its mailings. Publishers Clearing House had to stop this practice, and some of their other tactics. They can no longer use simulated checks or tell people in their mailings that the "Prize Patrol" is coming to their house. They've had to stop using phony and official looking stamps and seals on the entry forms with words like "prize affidavit" or "official document." The entry forms looked so "official" that many people thought they had won the sweepstakes. Under the settlement agreement Publisher Clearing House is now required to provide the odds of winning.

According to Carol, the Publishers Clearing House is not the only sponsor of a sweepstakes to come under scrutiny, but it is one of the most visible and highly publicized.

"I enter the Publisher Clearing House Sweepstakes every year and so far I haven't won, but that doesn't mean I've given up," she says, "Somebody has to win and I figure it might as well be me. I fully expect to see the "Prize Patrol" drive up my house someday!"

"As a devoted contester, I have found that winning can be fun, but I don't view my hobby as a get rich quick scheme," she says, "Just like anything else, planning and organization is an important part of the hobby. The trick isn't to find a contest or sweepstakes, because they are everywhere. The trick is to carefully give thought to the kind of contest or sweepstakes I want to enter because it's impossible to enter every one I come across. I try to be selective because the contesting landscape is constantly changing and I want to devote my time and effort to exactly the right contests or sweepstakes that appeals to me or my family. I also try to stay in a budget as to how much money to spend on stamps...I once read an article about a woman who sold her blood to get money for stamps for contesting!"

With this in mind, Carol made another attempt at conquering one of her longstanding challenges: making the cut for the Pillsbury Bake-Off Cooking Contest, which is also goal number nine on her new Dream List! Though she'd entered the contest countless times before, she'd never been chosen as one of the hundred finalists.

"I find there's something magical when I write down the goals I want to achieve and by writing them down I stay on course," she says. "It is important to set clear goals and know where you want to go and not be afraid of failure, which can be a redirection that leads to good things."

"Sometimes I think of how much different my life might have been if I'd never gotten into contesting," Carol muses, "I'm just a regular person from a little town in Illinois, but because of contesting I've been able to experience so much more than I would have otherwise, and have been able to win many of life's luxuries for my family and positively enrich their lives."

"Oscar Wilde once wrote, "Memory is the diary we all carry about with us," says Carol, "As I've recollected various memories for this book, I was surprised at how difficult it was to write about the people and relationships within my family... especially when I was a child. In doing so, I had to expose my own heart. As I wrote about the events in my life I came to realize that I hadn't let the circumstance and events that my sister and I were forced to deal with determine who I was. It doesn't matter how you begin in life; it's where you end up that matters and I was able to find strength because of the adversity. If I could handle growing up in a dysfunctional family, then I could handle anything!"

"This realization gave me the freedom to move forward and not be afraid. Also, I came to realize just how big a role contesting had influenced my life. *Need* was the catalyst responsible for my coming up with the creative actions I developed at an early age to win contests and sweepstakes."

"Life is a story, and I hope I have played my role with joy, enthusiasm, and a compassion for others," Carol recollects, "Not in my wildest dreams did I ever think I would grow up to travel the world, write a book, work as an extra in a Hollywood movie and be on the periphery of the movie industry, feel the warm rays of the equatorial sun on my head while visiting Fanning Islands, see my son carry the Olympic Torch, or anything else I've experienced."

"Albert Einstein summed up his life when he said, "There are only two ways to live your life: One is as though nothing is a miracle. The other is as though everything is a miracle." My life has truly been a miracle! My sister and I survived a childhood filled with fear and abuse caused by the illness of alcoholism...but we refused to let our spirits become crippled and atrophied. We chose instead to look to the future and get on with our lives and not dwell in the past."

"Helen Keller said, "Life is either a daring adventure or nothing." I've had a rich life full of adventure, wonderful children and grandchildren, and meaningful relationships with people I loved and my passion for contesting which helped me enjoy the journey!"

Carol's Tips:

"Be creative! If it is a contest or sweepstakes, I always try to do something that causes my entry to stand out and be noticed and different from all the other entries. I have found that contests and sweepstakes that have a short deadline offer a better chance for winning because there aren't as many entries. It seems like everyone is short of time these days (including me), so I try to utilize any spare time I have by filling out blanks while I watch television, wait in the waiting room of a doctor or dentist, while having my car serviced, etc. During vacation and Christmas time people are usually busy and don't enter as many contests or sweepstakes, so this is a good time to enter. The most lucrative contests and sweepstakes are those sponsored nationally rather than local, but these can be more difficult to win because there's more competition. I enter them all and have won in both arenas."

Ballot/ Draw Sweepstakes

1.) Boxes are usually displayed near the entrance of a store or near a specific product.
2.) Fan fold or crumble the entry blank before dropping it into the box to give the entry more body so it will be more likely picked out of the box.
3.) Fill out the entry with bright, colorful magic marker. (I carry magic markers in purse for this purpose).
4.) Bring some entry blanks home and soak them in water. After the entry dries fill it out and return the blank to the store. The entry blank will be stiff (paper gets stiff after it is wet and dries) and thus more apt to be chosen. Sometimes I will soak the entry in colored water to have a stiff, colorful entry. (I soaked an entry in green water in an attempt to win a trip to Ireland).
5.) Look for sweepstakes in slow traffic stores. (The odds of winning are greater because there won't be as many entries in

the box).

6.) Look for sweepstakes where there are more than one prize being offered and you will have a greater chance of winning something.

7.) If a chain store is sponsoring a sweepstakes try to enter at as many of the area stores as possible. (This helps to distribute your entries).

Mail-In Sweepstakes

1.) Judges look for contestants who follow the rules. (25% of entries are disqualified because contestants fail to follow the rules.) If the rules say print your name, then print it. If rules say only one entry per person, then only enter one entry. You can, however, send in entries for family members and friends. If the rules call for contestants to do a little legwork (such as looking for particular products at the store) do it because most people won't bother and your odds of winning increases. Be sure to read the rules to make sure the sweepstakes is legal in your state.

2.) Mail the entry in a colored envelope (unless the rules require that the entry be sent in a number10 white envelope). Save colorful envelopes from birthday cards (we never seal birthday cards but save the colorful envelopes for sweepstakes). Check with stationery or card shops. Sometimes they have inventory that they want to get rid of at little or no cost. Check with friends for their left over envelopes from Christmas cards they don't want.

3.) Decorate the entry and/or the envelope. Color gets results! Draw a picture on the entry blank that pertains to the sweepstakes. Use bingo dobbers or stickers to enhance the entry.

4.) If the rules call for a post card, decorate it. Picture post cards are effective because they are colorful and stand out.

5.) Decorate the entry with a picture cut from a magazine. Glue the entry on the blank.

6.) Spray the entry with perfume. (When the envelope is

opened the fragrance will get the entry noticed.)
7.) Pink the edge of an entry with pinking shears to give the blank a different feel.
8.) Laminate an entry blank for another look.
9.) Cover a large envelope with all one cent stamps postage.

Cooking Contests

1.) Give the recipe a catchy name.
2.) Prepare the recipe carefully. Give the right measurements for the ingredients and the right cooking time.
3.) Be sure to use the sponsor's product in the recipe.
4.) Use as few ingredients as possible. (People are very busy and like recipes that are fast and easy to prepare.)
5.) Use unusual ingredients, but ingredients that can be found in most grocery stores. (People don't want to be running around trying to find an exotic ingredient.)
6.) Experiment with a new flavor combination.
7.) Transform a main dish into an appetizer or a dessert into a snack.
8.) Explore own ethnic heritage and create a new shape or appearance for a family food.
9.) Substitute convenience ingredients for several ingredients in an old recipe.
10.) Test recipe on family and friends and ask for their feedback.
11.) Be aware of current food fads. (Study magazines and newly published cookbooks.)
12.) For an on site cooking contest, dress up in a costume that compliments the recipe. (If cooking Mexican food, dress up in Mexican attire.)
13.) If participating in a pie baking contest, time it so the pie is piping hot for the judging. (A hot pie taste better than a cold pie.)

Essay Contests

1.) Usually fewer contestants in an essay contest, so there is less competition.
2.) Make sure the words are spelled correctly.
3.) Make sure the essay is clear, to the point, and easily understood.
4.) Never copy an entry.
5.) Neatness counts! (Judges are turned off by ink smears or soiled paper).
6.) After the first draft, set the essay aside for a day or two. Then reevaluate the essay in an objective, super critical mAnnr.
7.) Mail the essay flat, backed by heavy cardboard.

Sources of Contests and Sweepstakes

1.) Newspapers (especially the Sunday paper)
2.) Magazines
3.) Television
4.) Radio
5.) Family
6.) Friends
7.) Managers, clerks, and vendors (people who deliver products) at stores.
8.) Store window displays
9.) Contest and sweepstakes newsletters
10.) In-store fliers
11.) The Internet
12.) Airline magazine (prize is usually a trip to the airline's destinations).
13.) Store grand openings
14.) Bulletin boards
15.) Warranty cards
16.) Product coupons (Look for sweepstakes on coupons and fill them out before redeeming).

17.) Your own mail-box (Publisher's Clearing House, Reader's Digest Sweepstakes, etc.)

Supplies

1.) Stamps (self-adhesive)
2.) Post cards (plain, pre-stamped, and an assortment of picture post cards).
3.) White stationery and envelopes.
4.) Colorful envelopes and stationery decorated with balloons, animals, flowers, etc. Can even make envelopes by using a regular number 10 envelope as a pattern and make colorful, eye-catching envelopes from heavy wrapping paper, stationery, or wallpaper.
5.) Assortment of pens (indelible ink is not apt to smear), pencils, and magic markers.
6.) Three by five inch index cards... white and colored. (If the store is out of entry blanks the sponsor of the sweepstakes usually allows an index card to be used as a substitute entry blank).
7.) Bingo markers of various colors.
8,) Colorful stickers.
9.) Magnifying glass (For reading the rules which are often in fine, hard to read print.)
10.) Pinking shears
11.) A shoe box to keep receipts (for tax deduction purposes) and for duplicate entries (for referring to the official rules after winning a specific contest or sweepstakes.)

List of Prizes Won

The following is a list of some of the prizes Carol has won for herself and her family, broken down by prize recipient.

Carol's Prizes

$10,000 Shopping Spree at Plaza Frontenac Mall (Sweepstakes drawing)
Trip to San Francisco, CA .
Trip to San Antonio, TX
Trip to Denver, CO
WOK (Won in a cherry pie baking contest).
$25 (Won in a cherry pie baking contest).
Smoker (Won in KMOX Radio Bar-B-Que Contest).
$100 (Grocery Store Drawing)
$25 (Best Meat Recipe Contest)
Oprah Winfrey's Guest (KSDK-TV mail-In a post card drawing).
River Cruise with radio announcer Jim White and wife Patty.
Nintendo Game (Wal-Mart Drawing).
Super Bowl Party (Schnuck's Store Drawing)
Breakfast with the Muni Opera Stars
$100 (National Foods Cooking Contest).
Cellular Telephone (Drawing at Venture Store)
Bread maker (Lorraine Cheese Sweepstakes Mail-In).
Christmas Turkey (Drawing at Bank).]
$25 (Fancy Feast Pet Food Drawing at Shop 'n Save).
2 Carat Diamond Necklace (Drawing at National Food Store).
Personal Alarm (Drawing at Target).
Safety Alarm (Drawing at Target)
4 St. Louis Cardinal baseball tickets (Schnuck's Store Drawing).
Two Jockey Duffel Bags (Drawing at J C Penney's).
Hawaii trip for 4 People ("Midwest Living Magazine" Contest).
$900 Golf Clubs (Part of the Hawaii Trip Contest)
$50 (Drawing at Target)
Polaroid Camera
Speaking part in the "KMOX Radio Holiday Show" at Westport Theater in St. Louis
$40 (Venture Drawing).
Collector Coins and $10 (Speech contest for Senator Ralph Dunn).
$500 Gift Certificate (Sears Drawing).

Winning Big

Las Vegas, NE trip for two
Dinner & video game playing with Rams Football Player, Marshal Falk (Tostitos Drawing)
Three 27 inch televisions (CBS "Answer the Questions" contest at Target Stores)
Las Vegas, NE trip for two (MLT essay contest about her mother).
32 inch television (Rothman Furniture Store Sweepstakes)
$3,300.34 (Contestant on the "To Tell The Truth" game show).
Two KMOV-TV "Count on Kent" umbrellas.
$50 (Wal-Mart drawing).
$50 (Wal-Mart drawing).
DVD movie (Dierberg Grocery Store drawing).
"Pearl Harbor" 60th Anniversary Commemorative DVD gift set (Grocery store drawing).
Suburban Journal Essay Contest (Wrote about China).
Pepsi Cola key chain belt (On-line sweepstakes).
Crystal Flute Wine Glasses valued at $120 (Drawing at Gordons Jewelry Store)
4 Tickets "Full Monty" at the Fox Theater (KMOV-TV Internet Sweepstakes)
Netties Flower Bouquet (KMOX Mail-In Sweepstakes)
$100 Gift Certificate at the Discovery ChAnnl Store (Chiquita Banana Sweepstakes)Autographed soccer Ball (Mail-In Sweepstakes)
4 Tickets "A Christmas Carol" at the Fox Theater (WIL Radio Internet Sweepstakes)
"Chanel Woman of Influence" Prize package/dinner at Coronado Ballroom (Essay Contest).
Beach Mat (Frito Lay Internet Sweepstakes)
Green Day $120 Giveaway (KMOV-TV Internet Sweepstakes).
$25 Shop 'N Save Gift Certificate (Winning Shopping Tip)
$50 "National Examiner" Essay Contest..."The Day That Changed My Life."
Won book "Entombed" (KEZK Radio Internet Sweepstakes)
4 Tickets "Disney On Ice" at the Savis Center (KMOV-TV Internet Sweepstakes).
2 Tickets "Working Woman's Survival Show" (Y-98 Radio Internet Sweepstakes).
CD (Y-98 Radio Internet Sweepstakes).
$50 Schnuck's Gift Card (Coca-Cola "Back to School" Mail-In Sweepstakes).

Winning Big

3 foot Holiday Bear (Coca-Cola Mail-In Sweepstakes).
Dinner for 4, gift boxes, and tickets to "Little Women" at the Fox (KEZK Sweepstakes).
42 bottles of 2 liter size soda (Coca-Cola Internet "Enter the Codes" sweepstakes).
Won book "Luckiest Man..The Life & Death of Lou Gehrig" (KEZK Internet Sweepstakes).
2 tickets "Mannheim Steamroller Show" at Scottrade Center (KMOV-TV Sweepstakes).
4 tickets "Sesame Street Live" & party with characters (KTVI-TV Internet Sweepstakes).
2 tickets "Speakers Series" CNN's Christiane Amanpour (KMOX Internet Sweepstakes).

Donna (Carol's oldest daughter)

Wristwatch (Drawing at Service Merchandise)
Diamond Ring (Drawing at Grand-Pa Pigeons).
Basketball (Drawing at K-Mart).
36 golf balls (Drawing at K-Mart).
Four Concert Tickets (Mail-In sweepstakes).
$25 (Meat recipe contest at The Market Place).
$100 Grocery Store Drawing.
Two Duffel Bags (J C Penney's Drawing).
$100 (Chrysler Dealership promotion).
Trip to a $400 per day Florida Resort (KMOX Radio Sweepstakes).
ChAnnl 4 "Monday Morning Make-Over (Essay Contest).
Day at a local health spa.
$50 Kraft Basket of Treats.
$75 Gift Certificate (Drawing at Dierbergs Markets).
Trip for 2 to Sydney, Australia for the Olympic games (Coca-Cola Sweepstakes).
Dodge Dealers "Football Toss" to try to win a Dodge truck.
2 tickets to attend a Missouri football game and a tailgate party.
Dinner for 2 to Outback Restaurant and Fernado Vina Baseball Camp (KEZK Internet).
$100 Gift Certificate (The Market Place Drawing).
Zatarain's Gift Box (Zatarian Internet Sweepstakes).
4 tickets to attend a St. Louis Cardinals baseball game (Schnuck's drawing)
4 tickets to ride the Forest Park Ferris Wheel (KSHE Radio Internet

Sweepstakes)
Free massage (Drawing at Rooster Health Food Store)
$3,000 Disney Trip to Florida (Tony's Pizza & WIL Radio Soccer Mom essay contest)
4 tickets to "Expresso" at The Fox Theater (KSDK-TV Internet Sweepstakes)
"Home Run Derby" at Busch Stadium (Schnuck's Mail-In Sweepstakes)
2 tickets to "Mama Mia" at The Fox (KMOV-TV Internet Trivia Contest)
Free haircut (Great Clips Sweepstakes)
$50 Gift Certificate (KEZK Radio Guarantee Contest)
$50 Schnucks Gift Card (Coca-Cola "Back to School" Mail-In Sweepstakes)
Holiday Bear (Coca-Cola Mail-In Sweepstakes)
$25 Dierberg Gift Certificate (Quaker Oats In-Store Drawing)
31 bottles (2 liter size) Coca-Cola (Package Code/Internet Contest).
Book (KEZK Internet Sweepstakes)
Prairie Farms Prize Package (Schnucks "Secret Shopper" Sweepstakes).
4 tickets "Les Miserables" at The Muni Opera and the Napoleon Exhibit (KMOX Sweepstakes)
4 St. Louis Cardinals baseball tickets (Digiorno Pizza "Slice of the Action" Sweepstakes)

Jim (Donna's husband)

Wristwatch (Drawing at Service Merchandise).
36 golf balls)Drawing at K-Mart).
Television (Drawing at Wal-Mart).
4 St. Louis Cardinal baseball tickets (Drawing at Wal-Mart).
St. Louis Blues Hockey "Play By Play" Participation (KMOX Mail-In Sweepstakes)
$40 Venture Gift Certificate (Drawing at Venture).
A Super Bowl Party (Schnucks Grocery Store Drawing).
Trip for 2 to Jamaica (Drawing at McDonald's Restaurant).
Free hair cut (Great clips Sweepstakes)

Amanda (Donna and Jim's daughter; Carol's eldest grandchild)

Eight foot Christmas sock filled with toys and games (Venture Store drawing).

4 concert tickets
2 videos (Schnucks coloring contest).
Personal alarm (Venture Store drawing).
$100 gift certificate for Discovery ChAnnl Store (Chiquita Banana Mail-In Sweepstakes)
Beach towel & blow up toy (Frito Lay Internet Sweepstakes).
2 tickets "Hairspray" at The Fox & $40 Bandanas gift certificate(Y-98 Internet Sweepstakes)
$50 Expo gift certificate & $20 certificate to Bob Evans Restaurant (KMOX Sweepstakes).
Beach Mat (Frito Lay Internet Sweepstakes)
"Home Run Derby" at Busch Stadium (Schnucks Mail-In Sweepstakes).
4 St.Louis Cardinals baseball tickets for 2005 season. (Schnucks drawing)
Free hair cut (Great Clips Sweepstakes)
$3,500 trip for 2 to VH1 Big End 2005 Awards in Hollywood (Y-98 Internet Sweepstakes)
$50 Schnucks gift card (Coca-Cola "Back to School" Mail-In Sweepstakes).
Holiday Bear (Coca-Cola Mail-In Sweepstakes).
2 tickets "Little Women" at the Fox (KEZK Internet Sweepstakes)
34 bottles (2 liter size) Coca-Cola (Package Code/Internet Sweepstakes).
"Home Run Derby" at Busch Stadium...2nd time to win it (Schnucks Mail-In Sweepstakes)

Nick Schoellhorn (Amanda's ex-boyfriend)

Autographed soccer ball (Chiquita Banana Mail-In Sweepstakes).
$500 (KATZ Radio Internet Sweepstakes).

Jimmy (Donna and Jim's son and Carol's grandson)

Eight foot Christmas sock filled with toys and games (Venture Store drawing).
4 concert tickets
Baseball and bat (K-Mart In-Store Drawing)
$50 bag of groceries (The Market Place In-Store Drawing)
Batman video (coloring contest).
Contestant for "Pillsbury Bake-Off For Kids" contest.
Rawling plastic batting machine (Nabisco Sweepstakes)

Paired with Cardinal player before game (Shop 'n Save "Kids Starting Line-Up")
Won trip to 1999 Final Four (Missouri Valley Free Serve Contest at Kiel Auditorium).
Won trip to 2002 Final Four (Missouri Valley Free Serve Contest at Savis Center).
Fuji Advantage Camera (Target "Bulls-Eye" Internet Sweepstakes).

Diana (Carol's youngest daughter)

$100 Circuit City Certificate
Camera
Cardinal Duffel Bag (J C Penney Drawing).
Olympic Sweatshirt (Target Mail-In Sweepstakes).
$40 Gift Certificate (Venture In-Store Drawing).
$75 Certificate for Michael's Craft Store (In-Store Drawing).
20 pounds of dog food (Pet Store Drawing).
Two Southwest Airline Tickets (Drawing at Wal-Mart).
KMOV-TV Monday Morning Make-Over (essay contest).
$150 Dierberg Certificate (Grocery Cart Race).
$300 Schnuck's Certificate (Dome Drop at TWA Stadium...caught 2 football parachutes).
Football Toss to win a Dodge truck. (Didn't win the truck but did receive a token prize prize).
"KMOX Exhausted Santa" Sweepstakes (won 4 movie tickets & $25 dinner certificate).
4 tickets "Bear in the Big Blue House" at Savis Center & $250 Value City Certificate).KMOX
Beach Towel (Frito Lay "Finding Nemo" Sweepstakes).
$100 Gift Certificate (Market Place Drawing).
$1,000 Bassett Furniture Certificate (Y-98 Internet Sweepstakes).
$5,000 Cabinet Refacing Certificate by St.Clair Construction (Y-98 Internet Sweepstakes).
Day at spa, Chanel products,$100 Famous-Barr("Chanel Woman of Influence" essay0.
4 tickets "Jesus Christ Superstar" at The Fox (Y-98 Internet Sweepstakes).
"Home Run Derby at Busch Stadium" (Schnuck's Mail-In Sweepstakes).
2 tickets to hear Jazz Ensemble at Umsul College (KMOX Internet Sweepstakes).

Winning Big

Free hair cut (Great Clips Sweepstakes).
$50 Schnucks Gift Card (Coca-Cola "Back to School" Sweepstakes).
4 tickets for "Ice Age" movie (KTVI-TV Internet Sweepstakes).
33 bottles (2 liter size) Coca-Cola (Package Code/Internet Contest).
2 tickets "Les Miserables" at The Fox (KEZK Internet Sweepstakes).
2 tickets Mama Mia at The Fox (KTVI-TV Internet Sweepstakes).
$75 certificate to Savazza Restaurant (KTVI-TV Internet Sweepstakes).
Prairie Farms Prize Package (Schnucks "Secret Shopper" Sweepstakes).
Digiorno Pizza Party with Cardinal Catcher Gary Bennett & Fred Bird (At her home).

Mark (Diana's husband)

St. Louis Blues Hockey "Play by Play (KMOX Mail in a post card sweepstakes).
4 St. Louis Cardinal Baseball tickets (Schnucks drawing).
Personal alarm (Target Store drawing).
Jockey Duffel Bag (J C Penney drawing).
Toy train collector's set.
Olympic Sweatshirt
Nintendo '64 game (Target Store drawing).
$2,000 Air Hockey Table (Coca-Cola Mail-In Sweepstakes).
$150 Dierberg Certificate (Grocery Cart race at TWA Dome at a Rams game).
Dodge Dealer's Football Toss to win Dodge truck (Didn't win truck.. got consolation prize).
Kellogg's Cookie recipe contest. (Mini football cookies)
Won night at Casino Queen Hotel & 2 meals (KMOV-TV Internet Sweepstakes).
2 St. Louis Cardinals baseball tickets (Schnucks mail-in sweepstakes).
Leather jacket)Drawing at his work).
$100 Schnucks Certificate (2 nd prize for Coca-Cola Football Getaway Sweepstakes).
Busch Stadium base keepsake (Schnucks "Run For History" Sweepstakes.
Free Hair Cut (Great Clips Sweepstakes).

Holiday Bear (Coca-Cola Mail-in Sweepstakes).

Ryan (Diana & Mark's son)

Baseball & Bat (K-Mart drawing).
Personal Alarm (Venture Store drawing).
Camera
Skateboard (The Athlete's Foot Drawing).
Nabisco Kids Starting LIne-Up at Busch Stadium (Shop'n Save Mail-In Sweepstakes).
St. Louis Cardinals Baseball Clinic & 4 game tickets (Brushito Mail-In Sweepstakes).
IPOD valued at $300 (Coca-Cola "Wanta Fanta" Sweepstakes)
2 "Old Busch" stadium seats valued at $400 (Schnuck's In-Store Sweepstakes).

Hannah (Diana & Mark's oldest daughter)

"Sylvester The Cat" valued at $150 (Bunny Bread drawing).
Personal alarm (Venture Store drawing).
Camera
4 Cardinal baseball tickets (Schnuck's drawing).
M & M Stuffed Toys (Bunny Bread drawing).
$25 (J C Penney coloring contest).
Barbie dolls (McDonald's Restaurant drawing).
Crate of toys & games (Universal Toys design a game board contest).
4 tickets to "MY Fair Lay" at The Muny & attended a tea (Won design a hat contest).
Won a video (Dierbergs coloring contest).
Free desserts for the family (Denney's Restaurant coloring contest).
Grand Marshal for Veiled Prophet Parade in St. Louis with Albert Pujols (Essay contest).
4 "Meet Me in St. Louis" tickets to Muny Opera (Poster contest about the musical).

Alynn (Diana & Mark's 2nd daughter)

Bugs Bunny valued at $150 (Bunny Bread drawing).
Won video (Dierberg coloring contest0.
$100 Dierberg gift certificate (In-store drawing).
Disney Collectors Bobble Heads (Kellogg Cereals sweepstakes).

Winning Big

4 tickets "Cinderella" & a tea at The Muny Opera (Designed a costume for Cinderella).
Autographed soccer ball (Chiquita Banana Mail-In Sweepstakes).
St. Louis Cardinal's baseball clinic & game tickets (Brushito Sweepstakes).
4 tickets "Cats" at The Muny (Won poster contest about the play "Cats").

Caroline (Diana & Mark's youngest daughter)

St. Louis Cardinals backpack and a Cardinal calculator (Coca-Cola Sweepstakes).
Legos & Twinkies (Twinkies Mail-in Sweepstakes).
4 tickets to a St. Louis Blues Hockey game (St. Louis Blues drawing & coloring contest).

Donald (Carol's son)

Television (In-store drawing at Grand-Pa Pigeons)
St. Louis Blues Hockey "Play By Play" participation (KMOX mail-in sweepstakes)
$1500 flooring gift certificate (Tile Town in-store drawing).
2 Jockey duffel bags (JC Penney's drawing).
4 St. Louis Cardinal baseball tickets (Schnucks drawing).
Ram's autographed football shirt (Ram's mail-in sweepstakes)
Superbowl party (Schnucks drawing).
Hockey stick & puck (K-Mart in-store drawing).
4 Southwest Airline tickets (Wal-Mart in-store drawing).
1999 "Basketball Shoot Out" at Kiel Auditorium (Schnucks mail-in post card).
Coca-Cola party for ten people (Coca-Cola Mail-In sweepstakes).
2000 "Basketball Shoot Out" at Kiel Auditorium (Schnucks mail in post card).
$300 Schnucks Gift Certificate ("Dome Drop" at TWA Dome...caught 2 football parachutes).
Dodge Dealer's "Football Toss" to try to win a truck... didn't win (Received consolation prize).
Tickets to Missou Football game and tailgate party. (Mail-In sweepstakes).
$200 Dierbergs Gift Certificate (In-store drawing).
Budweiser chair (Budweiser drawing).
Night at Casino Queen Hotel & 2 meals (KMOV-TV Internet

sweepstakes).
Autographed soccer ball (Chiquita Banana Mail-In sweepstakes).
Carried The Olympic Torch (Coca-Cola essay contest).
2 tickets to St. Louis Rams football game & opportunity to win $50,000 (Didn't win).
2 tickets to last baseball game at Busch Stadium (Mail-In Schnucks sweepstakes).
$300 IPOD (Coca-Cola "Wanta Fanta" sweepstakes).
2 tickets to see Cardinals play at new Busch Stadium (Schnucks drawing).
Free haircut ("Great Clips" Salons sweepstakes).
Holiday Bear (Coca-Cola mail-in sweepstakes).
2 tickets "Phantom of the Opera" at The Fox (KMOX Radio Mail-In sweepstakes).
34 bottles (2 liter size) Coca-Cola (Package Code/Internet contest).

Debra (Donald's wife & Carol's daughter-in-law)

$50 gift certificate at Wal-Mart (In-store drawing).
$40 gift certificate at Venture Store (In-store drawing).
Rams autographed football (Rams sweepstakes).
"Monday Morning Make-Over" (KMOV-TV essay contest).
2 Southwest Airline Tickets (Wal-Mart in-store drawing).
$100 U.S. Savings Bond (In-store drawing at Target Store).
Dodge Dealer's "Football Toss" to try to win a truck. Didn't win. (Received consolation prize).
Cooking lessons at Dierbergs Cooking School.
Bar-B-Que grill (Dierbergs drawing).
Hammock (Drawing at Schnucks).
Crystal Flute Wine Glasses valued at $120 (Drawing at Gordons Jewelery Store).
Radio cooler valued at $100 (Budweiser mail-in drawing).
$100 Dierbergs gift certificate (In-store drawing).
4 tickets to "the Carlos Santana Show" (Y-98 Radio Internet sweepstakes).
Night at Casino Queen Hotel & 2 meals (KMOV-TV Internet sweepstakes).
4 tickets to see "A Christmas Carol" at The Fox (KMOX Radio Internet sweepstakes).
$2800 trip for 2 to Jupiter, FL Cardinal's Spring Training (KMOV-TV Internet sweepstakes).

Free massage (Rooster Health Food Store sweepstakes).
2 tickets "Meet Me In St. Louis" at The Muny (KMOX Radio Internet sweepstakes).
$75 American Express Card & prize package ("The Point" Radio Internet sweepstakes).
"Green Day" Giveaway $120 prize package (KMOV-TV Internet sweepstakes).
Michael Payne Seminar "Designing For The Sexes" (KEZK Internet sweepstakes).
$50 gift certificate (Tony's Pizza & WIL Radio "Soccer Mom" essay contest).
"Home Run Derby" at Busch Stadium (Schnucks sweepstakes).
"Final Four" party (Schnucks in-store sweepstakes).
$300 IPOD (Coca-Cola "Wanta Fanta" sweepstakes).
2 tickets Cardinals game & batting practice with Ricky Horto (Schnucks drawing).
2 Dr. Phil books (Y-98 Radio Internet sweepstakes).
$25 Dierbergs gift certificate (In-store drawing).
Free haircut ("Great Clips" Salons sweepstakes).
4 tickets Ringling Brothers Circus (Famous Barr Department Store drawing).
Holiday Bear (Coca-Cola mail-in sweepstakes).
4 tickets Ray Ramaro Show at The Fox (KEZK Internet sweepstakes).
"Home Run Derby" at Busch Stadium ISchnucks sweepstakes)

David (Donald & Debra's oldest son & Carol's grandson)

Go-Cart (Drawing at Arnold Wal-Mart Store)
$100 & birthday party supplies (Elmo's sweepstakes at party supply store).
$100 U.S. Savings Bond (Dodge Van Dealership promotion).
Nabisco "Starting Line-Up" at Busch Stadium (Nabisco/Shop 'n Save sweepstakes).
Lessons at Cardinal's baseball clinic/ 4 tickets to a game (Brushito Cheese sweepstakes).
Busch Stadium baseball camp (Schnucks mail-in sweepstakes).

Drew (Donald & Debra's younger son & Carol's grandson)

St. Louis Cardinals Back-Pack and matching Cardinal calculator.
4 tickets St. Louis Blues hockey game (St. Louis Blues coloring

contest).
Nabisco "Starting Line-Up" at Busch Stadium (Nabisco/Shop 'n Save sweepstakes).
"Walk With The Dinosaurs" show" at Savis Center (KTVI-TV Internet sweepstakes).

Prizes Carol won for Edward Reinbold & his family

Trip for two to the 2004 Olympics in Athens, Greece (Coca-Cola in-store sweepstakes)
$150 Gift Certificate for Michael's Craft Store (In-store drawing).
Case of root beer (Vogts IGA Grocery Store drawing).
4 Muny Opera tickets (KMOX mail-in sweepstakes).
4 St. Louis Cardinals tickets to Busch Stadium (Schnucks mail-in sweepstakes).
$50 IGA Gift Certificate (In-store drawing at Vogts IGA Grocery Store).
$50 Schnucks Gift Certificate (Schnucks mail-in drawing).
2 Tickets to any show at The Fox (Mail-in post card to KMOX).
7 day Caribbean cruise on The Carnival Cruise Ship "Destiny" (Mail-in sweepstakes).
$2500 trip to "The Superbowl" (Mail-In Sweepstakes).
4 St. Louis Cardinals baseball tickets to Busch Stadium (Schnucks mail-in sweepstakes).
St. Louis Blues Hockey Shirt (St.Louis Blues mail-in sweepstakes).
4 St. Louis Cardinals baseball tickets to Busch Stadium (Dierbergs in-store drawing).
Stuffed Bugs Bunny valued at $150 (Bunny Bread drawing).
$50 Dierbergs Gift Certificate (Mail-in post card sweepstakes).
Cardinal party for ten people at Busch Stadium (Coca-Cola mail-in sweepstakes).
$2800 trip to San Diego, Ca (Shell Service Station drawing).
$500 Branson, Mo trip to see "The New York Rockettes" (Shop 'n Save mail-in post card).
5 Miller Beer blow up chairs valued at $500 (Miller Beer drawing).
DVD (In-store drawing at Dierbergs).
Schnucks $25 Gift Certificate (Durkee Spices mail-in sweepstakes).
Pearl Harbor 60th Anniversary Commemorative DVD Gift Set (KEZK Internet sweepstakes).
Underwater Camera (Mail-in Chiquita Banana sweepstakes).
Trip to Kansas City to a St. Louis Rams football game (Coors Beer

mail-in sweepstakes)
$200 Dierbergs Gift Certificate (In-store sweepstakes).
$50 Valentine shaped box of candy (Dierbergs Internet sweepstakes).
4 tickets Chase-Park Cinemas, 4 Idaho potatoes, and 2 shirts (KMOX Internet sweepstakes).
Beach towel & blow up toy (Frito-Lay Internet sweepstakes).
8 Great Plains Airline Travel vouchers (KMOX "Travel Tips" contest on the Internet).
4 St. Louis Rams "Bobble Heads" (KTVI-TV Internet sweepstakes).
2 underwater cameras (Dannon Spring Water mail-in sweepstakes).
4 tickets to "Jesus Christ Superstar" at The Fox (Y-98 Internet sweepstakes).
Trip to 2004 Olympics at Athens, Greece (Coca-Cola drop-in-a-box sweepstakes).
Green Day giveaway $120 prize package (KMOV-TV Internet sweepstakes).
Dinner for 4 at the Mississippi Queen Gambling Boat (KMOV-TV Internet sweepstakes).
33 bottles (2 liter size) Coca-Cola (Package Code/Internet sweepstakes).
2 tickets to see Johnny Mathis at The Fox (KMOX Internet sweepstakes).

Jo Ann (Carol's sister)

Toy car (Drawing at The Market Place).
$25 Wal-Mart Gift Certificate (In-store drawing).
4 tickets "Disney On Ice" (KMOV-TV Internet Sweepstakes).
4 St. Louis Cardinals baseball tickets to Busch Stadium (Schnucks drawing).

Bob (Jo Ann's husband)

4 St. Louis Cardinals baseball tickets to Busch Stadium (Schnucks drawing).
2 Southwest Airline tickets (Wal-Mart In-store drawing).
Television (Mail-in post card to Target Stores).
Autographed soccer ball (Chiquita Banana mail-In sweepstakes).
"Green Day" prize package valued at $120 (KMOV-TV Internet sweepstakes).

4 St. Louis Cardinals Baseball Tickets to Busch Stadium (KMOX Mail-In sweepstakes).

Tony (Bob & Jo Ann's son & Carol's nephew)

$50 (Valvoline Car Photo Contest...sent photo of Tony's purple car).
Robot car (Wal-Mart in-store sweepstakes).

Erika (Bob & Jo Ann's granddaughter)

"Kids Starting Line-Up" at Busch Stadium, 4 baseball tickets (Nabisco Mail-In sweepstakes).
Cardinal Baseball Camp & 4 tickets to a Cardinal game. (Brushito Cheese sweepstakes).

Emily (Bob & Jo Ann's granddaughter)

Cardinal Baseball Camp & 4 tickets to a Cardinal game. (Brushito Cheese sweepstakes).

Don Shaffer (ex-husband)

LHS Chrysler Car (Sherwin Williams Paint Store drop-in-a-box sweepstakes).
4 St. Louis Cardinals baseball tickets (Schnucks in-store sweepstakes).
Honorary manager for St. Louis Cardinals team (Upper Deck Baseball Cards sweepstakes).
Sharp ballpoint pen (Grand-Pa Pigeons in-store sweepstakes).
$100 Vogts Gift Certificate (Vogts IGA in-store drawing).
$40 Target Gift Certificate (Target mail in post card sweepstakes).
"Superbowl Party" (Schnucks drawing).
2 Nascar tickets (Shop' n Save mail-in sweepstakes).
Football beanbag chair (The Market Place in-store sweepstakes).
Golf umbrellas (Chrysler dealership sweepstakes).
Instant camera (Fuji sweepstakes).

About the Author:

Colin J. Mitchell is a graduate of the Broadcast Journalism program at Mohawk College of Applied Arts & Technology and a former staff writer for the college newspaper, *The Satellite*. The lifelong Hamilton resident is also a prolific professional freelance writer and editor. *Winning Big* is his first book.

Winning Big

Manor House Publishing
www.manor-house.biz.
905-648-2193

www.ingramcontent.com/pod-product-compliance
Lightning Source LLC
Chambersburg PA
CBHW021103080526
44587CB00010B/359